D1538711

/THEATER iN MY HEAD

dan cheifetz

/theater in my head

PHOTOGRAPHS BY NANCY HELLEBRAND

LITTLE, BROWN AND COMPANY   BOSTON TORONTO

*Published simultaneously in Canada
by Little, Brown & Company (Canada) Limited*

PRINTED IN THE UNITED STATES OF AMERICA

This book is respectfully dedicated to the person whose generosity made possible the workshop at the Metropolitan Duane United Methodist Church. Although I have never met her and she prefers to remain anonymous, her actions reflect a person with a rare and selfless concern for the lives of children.

. . . *time is granted to the child to exchange a spiritual connection with the world he gradually loses.* . . . *But he does not possess it yet; he must first draw it truly out, he must make it into a reality for himself, he must find for himself his own world by seeing and hearing and touching and shaping it. Creation reveals, in meeting, its essential nature as form.*

— Martin Buber, *I and Thou*

I wish to acknowledge with thanks the help of the following, who read the manuscript and made many valuable suggestions: Margaret Cheifetz, Joyce Baron of the Rockland Project School, Barbara Leavy and Amy Miller of Columbia Teachers College, and Howard Fussiner. A special acknowledgment is due for the help of the late and much missed Shifra Nathan. Shifra loved children just the way they were, and her enthusiasm for them, and for the work I was doing with them, is part of the animating spirit of this book.

/ CONTENTS

Illustrations appear between pages 81 and 98.

/THEATER IN MY HEAD

1 / THE GAME'S THE THING

The children straggled into the small gym by ones and twos. Some, those who had come with a friend or a sibling, eyed the singles and whispered together. One girl stood near the entrance and vigorously scratched her arms and legs and sometimes her back. A neatly dressed boy came in and went to a corner of the gym. He stood exactly where the side and back walls met, slouching and staring solemnly at his shoes. Another boy picked up a basketball that was lying around and shot a basket. His friend got the rebound and dribbled away. Two girls went up on the stage that occupied the far end of the gym and began to play house. One served tea to the other, using a battered table and bench that were there. The high-ceilinged gym was drafty and the heating system occasionally made clinking and sighing noises.

So began my workshop in dramatic play and learning. The children, ten girls and five boys, aged eight to eleven, were to meet thirteen successive Saturday mornings for an hour and a half at the Metropolitan Duane United Methodist Church in New York City. I liked the physical setup. There was room enough for the children to play and perform but not so much space that it would be difficult to round them up and concentrate them in one place when necessary.

I gathered them together now, asking them to sit on the floor around me. They dawdled on the way, reluctant to start, or rather, pretending elaborate coolness about the whole affair. Finally they sat, keeping careful distances between themselves and anyone they didn't know; at the same time, they stole curious glances at one another. I told them very briefly about what we were going to do in the workshop: play pretend games, act out things, pantomime, improvise (I explained that) and other activities that I hoped would be fun and also help them learn.

I asked them to stand up if they knew the game Simon Says. They all stood up. I said this would not be the usual "put your right hand on your left shoulder" kind of Simon but a Simon who would turn them into all different kinds of creatures. I would be Simon first, then give them a chance to be Simon.

"Simon says, 'Spread out and give yourself lots of room.'" They did.

"Simon says, 'Be a tightrope-walker!'"

The boy who had stood by himself in the corner before we had begun now was standing directly in front of me. He threw his arms out at right angles to his torso and planted his left foot carefully behind himself. Slowly he swung his right foot around and placed it at a slightly toed-out angle directly in front of himself, his whole body wavering and swaying in a well-imagined move-and-countermove struggle with gravity. He brought his left foot around, then the right, then more quickly the left again. He stopped, almost fell, righted himself, and got set to move forward again.

This was Brent, a ten-year-old black boy from a Chelsea tenement. He certainly did not look like the same boy who had slumped in a corner, staring at his feet. Now he stood as tall as he was, a poised and graceful figure, his eyes wide open in concentration on an inner world in which he was fifty feet off the ground while thousands held their breath beneath.

"Simon says, 'Be a snake!'"

Immediately Brent was off the swaying tightrope and onto his stomach, hissing and writhing on the floor. Another snake, a leggy, pretty, eleven-year-old white girl named Sally, hissed at him. Brent blinked at her, hesitated, then hissed back, hard. Sally smiled delightedly and hissed again. Then both stared at an entirely different creature, not a snake at all, but a person playing on a pipe and rolling her eyes. This was Margie, an imp-faced black girl of nine. Simon couldn't tell *her* what to do. She had decided not to *be* a snake but to *control* one. A sinister cobra was rising on the mysterious music of her pipe. It was Margie's friend, nine-year-old Joyce, wearing a colorful robozo, short pigtails and a Mona Lisa smile. Her tongue-fangs flicked in and out and her head turned like a pig-tailed searchlight, looking for a victim to strike.

But before she could find one, Simon had said, "Be a monster!"

Cobra forgotten, Joyce rose and clumped about, neck and face rigid as a monster, but arms held out more like a scarecrow. Suddenly, a girllike squeal came from her, and she ducked away. A light-haired boy monster, ten-year-old

Stan, was approaching fast. Actually, monster Stan had not been after Joyce but his friend, monster Richard (my son, a curly-haired nine-year-old). The two Frankensteins clutched each other and prepared for a squeeze-each-other-to-death match.

But, just in time, Simon had said, "Be pigs!"

And Stan and Richard were in the mud together, snuffling and oinking. Richard turned over on his back, bent his hands slightly at the wrist, held his legs stiff in the air, and rolled luxuriously from side to side. For a blinding instant, boy and pig were one.

A plump, auburn-haired, ten-year-old named Sandy was watching him. A while before, when we were sitting together in a circle, she had been at the edge of the group. Now she was laughing at Richard's piggish roll in the mud. Then she leaned against the gym wall and began to rub her back against it, up and down, back and forth, her eyes closed in piglike pleasure. But not for long.

"Simon says, 'Be a dog!' "

Sandy went to her hands and knees, then her haunches. She had been the one scratching herself when the other children had wandered in. Now she incorporated her nervous habit into her role: she vigorously scratched her fleas!

Near her was a frightened-looking boy dog, a towhead named Donald, who had just turned eight. Throughout the game, Donald had been copying the actions of his ten-and-a-half-year-old sister Stacey, as if we had been playing Follow the Leader instead of Simon Says. Suddenly his sister bounded away across the gym to chase a rabbit. Donald tried to follow but his way was blocked by a big mastiff with bared teeth. This was Carrie, a sullen-looking black girl of eleven. The big dog barked threateningly at the little one. The pup tried to bark back but his opponent was so big and fierce, tears came instead. Seeing his distress, his big sister left the rabbit chase and came bounding back to the rescue. But just as she arrived, the mastiff had reared up and become a light-footed vision of gentle grace who wouldn't have hurt one of Sandy's fleas. Tricky Simon had commanded: "Be a ballet dancer!"

No question about it, a game's the thing to get children involved in a new activity. Their desire to have fun playing the game overcame their social anxiety. Once they got into it, this game generated its own security and belongingness. When they were inside the game, they were inside the group, and so could relax their fears.

And as with any game, the rules were automatically accepted. No wildness and little silliness cropped up, because playing the game by the rules is self-disciplining. The children themselves would handle any unruly player who disturbed the ritual of playing.

Playing this special kind of game also helped overcome the children's reluctance to commit themselves to this new group, because it helped define the nature of the group. It wasn't a class or a club; what was it? Simon and his magic transformations began to answer that question. He also made it fun to be part of the group, *whatever* it was. And seeing one another do interesting and funny things was a good way to satisfy their curiosity about one another.

Other things were happening too. Take Brent again. Just by looking at him gracefully defying death on that high wire, one could see how much he was involved in what he was doing. His whole body, and his inner sense of his body, were involved in an imaginative re-creation of how physical equilibrium is maintained, lost, and then found again. His memories came into play: he must have seen such an artist in an actual circus or on television.

And maybe his own private dreams of glory, as well, were represented on that high wire.

Children often pretend to be someone more powerful or heroic than themselves in their private fantasies. The difference is that, perhaps for the first time, Brent had a chance to *become* his fantasy in the flesh. And he had moved his fantasy out of himself and into public view.

So often a child meets with a patronizing attitude, or even contempt, if he reveals his secret life to adults. Normally, Brent would have been afraid of being laughed at if someone "caught" him pretending to be a high-wire artist, or acting out any other cherished dream or weird story he might have told himself. If his fantasies are held in low esteem by the adults who guide him and whose love and acceptance he needs, he cannot possibly esteem them very highly himself. He will more likely feel guilty about them. He will wall off his acceptable "real life" from his secret, made-up one.

But on that imagined high wire, Brent's fantasy life and real life become one. By encouraging him to play out his fantasy, and by praising his public expression of it, we can begin to break down the psychic wall between his "real life" and his secret one. In this way, his secret fantasies become more available to him as a source of creative power in his everyday life, rather than a part of himself to feel guilty about and reject.

Children are often made uneasy by adult questions like: "What are you going to be when you grow up?" Or: "What do you like to do the most?" Though they are natural role-players and experimenters, such questions and the attitude they represent may make children feel they would be more acceptable and loved if they could more clearly define themselves: as an aspiring fireman or nurse, or someone who likes only to play marbles or draw pictures.

It may persuade them to find safety and definition in a single role, or in a very limited number of roles, and discourage them from trying new ones. Experience in role-playing, such as our game of Simon Says, helps counteract this pressure to specialize too early and validates the child's natural inclination to experiment. Another benefit is that by trying on different roles — like hats, to see if they fit — a child may discover elements in himself he did not know were there.

A boy like Brent, who sits himself in a corner to wait for someone's instruction before he moves, probably never thought of himself as poised or graceful or brave. But he could not be so skillful playing a high-wire artist unless he too had some of these gifts. This role is a way for him to discover new qualities in himself that his everyday life might never have given him the opportunity to sense.

Simon changed Brent and the other children into snakes and dogs and monsters, as well as heroic tightrope-walkers. To portray each role, the child had to identify, however imperfectly, with a creature completely different from himself. He had to seek in his own imagination and experience for some inner connection, some understanding, of such a creature. Since he has identified with it, he may thereby be motivated to find out more about it. Certainly he has stretched his general capacity to identify and imagine.

9

2 / Caviar to the Specific

Stan and Richard were onstage, pantomiming a certain common household action. When they finished, I asked who could describe what the boys had been doing. Several raised hands and I nodded to Joyce, the cocoa-colored cobra of Simon Says.

"Joyce, can you come up front and tell us what they were doing?"

She made a face at having to come up, but she came.

"Painting something," she said. I looked at the boys and they nodded she was right.

"Good. Now what do you think they were painting?"

She hesitated and said, "Table or chair or something."

"Table," said Stan.

"Fine. Now, Joyce, can you think of some ways they

could have made it clearer to us that it was a table and only a table they were painting?"

"Well," she said. "It would be better if they had a real table. Like that one over there." She pointed to the large ink-stained wooden table in the corner.

I smiled and said yes, it would have been clearer with a real table, but wasn't it more fun to pretend one and make us guess, rather than give it away by using a real one?

It was only later that I realized that my comment did not really fit the quality of her answer. This was Joyce's first exposure to the "creative" approach and she was expressing her confident belief in the superiority of the tangible over the merely pretend. And because her answer was so direct and unconditioned, it had a radical quality to it: it went to the root of the matter. Why indeed is it better to pretend a table when a real one is available? When there is so much children must learn about the real world, what is the advantage of making up an imaginary one? True, they love to pretend and they have fun doing it — a benefit in itself. But this was a workshop for learning too. The boys were being "creative," but creative in what way, for what purpose?

The painting of the table was part of a second activity I had begun with them, a group pantomime.

"We're going to give a big party," I had told them, "and we need everyone to help."

I asked for volunteers for each of the tasks: dusting, vacuuming, making beds, shopping, cooking, picking flowers and putting them in vases, painting furniture. I had to think up some alternatives: no one wanted to wash windows, for instance, but several wanted to vacuum the rug. Some wanted to work alone, some in small groups, but everyone chose a project and took some space to rehearse it. The idea was for them to practice their activity and then do it for the group, if they wished. The group would then try to guess the activity in detail.

I went from group to group to note progress and to help if necessary. First I visited the flower-pickers: Brent, the tightrope-walker of Simon Says, and Donald, the dog who had quailed before the fierce mastiff. Both had volunteered to gather the flowers. Watching them now, the dark head next to the light one, not speaking to each other but each bent to his task, I was struck by two things at once: their intense involvement in what they were doing, and the generalized way they were doing it. Certainly they were picking something, but there was no way of knowing what it was.

Both said they had picked flowers before. Neither, however, had firmly in mind the particular flowers they were picking now. I asked them to choose a type of flower to pick, and then remember how it actually felt to pick it. How that flower had a soft but crisp stem, just so big; how it was rooted in the earth and didn't want to leave, so you had to pluck it firmly; but since it was beautiful and you wanted to hurt it as little as possible, you had to pluck it gently. Most important, I said, remember how you felt inside yourself when you picked flowers. Think how you feel when you pick up some dirt, or a ball, or even a weed, and then remember the *different* way you feel when you pick a flower.

They tried it again. I could see their hands become a little more sensitive. The expression on their faces changed too. They were looking inside, remembering how it was, and giving back some of their true actions and feelings. Later, when they did it in front of the group, their self-consciousness made them revert to frozen faces and stiff fingers. They were mostly anxious to get finished and get off. But I had seen something happen, small as it was, when we had worked together, and I knew what they were capable of doing.

I moved on to some shoppers and the storekeeper waiting on them. The shoppers were bustling about, pulling many items from the shelves and filling their baskets. But as I watched them, I was again struck by the contrast between the fullness of enthusiasm and energy and the sparseness of authentic detail or variation of gesture. The monotony and unexactness of their actions surprised me more than that of the boys picking flowers. Donald's and Brent's experience with flowers was limited, but I was sure these girls had shopped themselves, or had accompanied their mothers many times to the store, and so were well versed in all the mysteries of the process.

"What are you buying there, Carrie?" I asked the fierce mastiff of Simon Says.

"Caviar," she said rather defensively.

"Jar? Can? Small size? Jumbo?"

"A *little* can. Don't you know that's all I can spend?"

"All right," I said. "Now take a can of caviar off the shelf, and show me that it *is* a little can." She showed me and the item took on an exact shape and weight. "Very good. Now, put it back and start over, and remember that you're worried about spending too much and want to make very sure you're getting the best buy. Shop around, look at the prices on other cans and jars before you choose. Isn't that what you'd do if you were in a store?"

She nodded and as I watched, a thrifty housewife with knit brows came into being, the various shapes and sizes and weights of jars and cans coming into focus in her empty hand.

The groceress, a plump ten-year-old white girl with merry eyes and wildly curly hair named Betty, was ring-ing up a customer's purchases. She punched her keys furiously, wrote something down, put something in a bag.

"Where did you get the bag?" I asked her.

"From this pile," she said coolly.

"I didn't see you pick it up or snap it open. Can you do another one?"

She picked a bag off a pile and made a mini-gesture with it.

"That little bag going to be enough for everything in her basket?"

"It's a great big bag!" she protested.

"Well, let's see it!"

Using both hands this time, she grasped the giant bag she had in mind and snapped it open with a movement that meant business. At the same time she made a loud "Pow!" with her mouth. She set the bag proudly on the counter.

"Now that's a bag!" I exclaimed. "All right, now one thing at a time, and be careful of those eggs."

Carrie, the big girl with the caviar taste, came up to me with something about three and a half inches in diameter, indicated between thumb and forefinger.

"See what I'm going to buy?" she said.

"Your husband must have gotten a raise or something. That's a pretty big can of caviar."

"Not *caviar*," she said scornfully. "It's tuna! It's cheap — see? — and there'll be more for the kids at my party to eat!"

I continued on my route, next watching Stan and Richard rehearse painting a table. But they had no discernible bucket in which to dip their brushes — or, rather, it appeared wherever they were. The paint would have been dripping all over the surface, since neither of them remembered to drain the excess paint from his brush by touching it to the rim of the can. And they could have been painting almost anything from a house to a baseball field. After a few moments of reminding them of their actual painting experiences, and of what they knew of tables, something much more recognizable began to take shape.

So it went. Robin, an eight-year-old who was the official soupmaker, merely kept stirring her paddle around and around, until we talked about how her mother peels and puts different vegetables into the kettle, stirs the mixture, tastes it, salts it, and so on. The vacuum cleaner at first was just a small clenched fist going back and forth, although nine-year-old Lucy did remember to unplug and replug the machine when she went from one room to another.

It was exciting to see the difference between the raw work the children had begun with and what most of them did after I had spent a little time working with them. But the question is, why did they have such initial difficulty in reproducing with any exactness ideas, objects and actions common to their own experience and observation?

I can only speculate. When these children were babies and toddlers, they spent uncounted hours exploring their environment — grabbing it, biting it, breaking it; watching it, listening to it, throwing it around; feeling its temperatures and textures; crawling into, under, over and around everything in sight. This rage to explore, and all the learning that takes place because of it, is one reason why they made such strides in their intellectual development.

But now that they have reached school age, their sensory learning is on the wane. For one thing, the repeated dictum "Don't touch!" has gotten to them. For another, the important adults in their lives, who used to express their delight with: "Watch him push that ball!" now pridefully ask their friends to "Listen to him read!" In fact, almost all their learning, now a formal rather than a spontaneous process, has become verbal, symbolic and conceptual in nature. Each thing has a name, a definition, a set of properties, all of which they have to learn, and all in words. They are urged to make the thing theirs by mastering its verbal concepts; they would then be able to talk about it, get good grades on tests by using the concepts correctly, and base other knowledge on such mastery.

It goes without saying that verbal and conceptual learning is an integral part of a child's intellectual development. The problem is that with the emphasis so heavy on learning through words and symbols, the information that comes to these children through eyes, fingers, ears, toes and tongue, is unconsciously downgraded or ignored by them. The lack of detail in the children's pantomimes reflected not indifference to the activity, and not self-consciousness, but vagueness about real things and actions.

So, in that case, isn't Joyce right? Wouldn't it be better to supply the boys with a real table? The answer is no, because if I had, they would have paid no attention to it!

They know its name, the names of its parts and materials, and its classification. That's all they need to know. However, to ask them to create a table through movement and gesture in thin air, to motivate them to get across to an audience that this is a table and nothing but a table — that is something else again. Then they might be nudged out of their contentment with abstract knowledge and be forced to rediscover *tableness itself.*

To "perform" a table — or a can of caviar (or tuna) or a flower or the running of a vacuum cleaner — the child must wake up his senses and perceive the object. If he really means to communicate it, he will pay attention to and remember the smallest detail and action involved. It only seems paradoxical to say that a child can learn a great deal about concrete reality by pretending objects and ideas. Actually, this kind of activity is a good way to make the world less fuzzy to a child, to increase his ability to think clearly about it, and to motivate him to be more accurate in his personal interpretation of it.

It is also a good way to increase a child's self-esteem, since this kind of activity encourages him to perform his own vision of reality. An actual table is common to all and visible to all; only the table the child creates with gesture and movement is his own. The actual table limits his imagination, while the one he makes up frees an image seen only in his inner eye. Performing this vision for others, and getting the satisfaction of their recognizing it, not only as a table, but *his* table, cannot help but make him feel good about himself.

There is also ancient magic in pretending, a transforming power that can make dreams come true. In some tribes, before boys were allowed to hunt with the men, they were required to learn and then exactly perform the ritual pantomime of the successful kill. When they did so, their dream of manhood came true.

Dreams come true if a child believes in what he is pretending. When Brent was rehearsing the gathering of his flowers, Nancy Hellebrand, the photographer for this book, came over and asked him if he would give her some. She told him she loved flowers. Brent didn't look up at her, only shook his head shyly and continued picking. Nancy didn't insist.

When the session was over and Nancy was about to

leave, Brent rushed up to her breathlessly and said, "Wait! You forgot your flowers!"

He presented her with a whole armload of the flowers of his imagination, then ran upstairs like the wind to meet his mother.

3/ Rhythm of the Rope

I said to them, "We worked very hard getting ready for that party last week. It was a big smash and we've earned some fun. So, let's skip rope!"

The boys didn't like the idea too much, though it helped when I reminded them that prizefighters and even football players skip rope to keep in shape. The girls, of course, were more willing.

"Here, Robin, you're a turner," I said to the eight-year-old soupmaker of our party-preparation pantomime, giving her the end of an imaginary jump rope. "Betty, you take the other end. Everyone else line up and take a turn jumping."

The girls lined up, though they seemed uncertain about how it would work. What's the fun of skipping rope without a rope? The boys loitered at the end of the line, or else took up independent positions a little to one side.

Robin began to turn with great energy, but in huge erratic circles. Betty, a rebel at ten years old, with unregimented masses of honey-colored hair, stuck one indifferent foot in front and one in back, placed her right arm akimbo, and turned in small, loose-wristed circles with her left.

"Ever skip rope?" I asked her.

She looked at me as though I were crazy. "Sure!"

"Well, from the way you're turning, I wondered."

But my intervention was not necessary. The other girls wanted to get on with it. Several of them told Betty to "get going." Robin was beginning to turn in smaller arcs and with greater regularity and told Betty to please get together with her. Sighing at their uncool attitude, Betty slowly shifted to the stance she must have taken a hundred times in the past: legs somewhat apart, torso squared away and slightly leaning toward her partner. Her right hand remained on her hip, however, as she and Robin maneuvered to find a common turning rhythm. Finally, the invisible rope began coming around slowly and steadily.

"Jump in when you're ready there, first person," I said.

Margie jumped in without preliminaries and hopped up and down a few times without reference to anything.

"Oh, you're out," Betty said. Margie shrugged, put her nose in the air, and made a face that said, "Who cares about such a silly thing anyway!"

The next girl was Sandy, the plump, uncertain girl given to scratching herself. Probably she felt awkward and heavy-footed when she skipped rope with other children, or more likely, avoided such games altogether. Now, she didn't jump in at all but only moved up to where the make-believe rope was coming around and went through the motions of jumping in time. Her concern was only to get her turn over with and fade back into the group. I started to say something, but restrained myself and let them go on.

Next was Stacey, Donald's older sister, a graceful, pretty girl who went to a progressive school. She didn't jump in right away, but began nodding time with her head and torso, until she felt the moment to move had come. She jumped in just right, but jumped again almost immediately, several seconds before the rope had a chance to come around.

The girl behind her said, "Hey, you're out!"

Stacey frowned, shook her head at herself, and stepped aside. But she had succeeded in recalling to their minds how you needed to adjust yourself to the beat of a turning rope in order to jump in right and to continue jumping successfully. Her successor, long-legged, long-haired Sally, who had a breathless, wide-eyed manner, raised both her forearms and beat time with them until she felt she had discovered the exact timing of the cycle. Then she jumped in, waited a count of four, jumped again, and again, and again, watching Betty's turning left hand carefully all the while.

I glanced at the other children after Sally's first successful jumps. All of them were watching her, unconscious of themselves. All of them were empathically beating time. My eleven-year-old daughter Amy twitched to the right each time her friend Sally jumped. Joyce rhythmically bent at the knees, up and down, at each jump. Others tapped their feet or nodded their heads. For the first time, someone had mastered the rope and the beat had entered them all.

After seven or eight good jumps, Sally felt herself get

entangled in the rope and jumped aside. Her large brown eyes looked triumphant. The next girl, Lucy, turned out to be a quiet virtuoso. She jumped in well, hopped neatly on two feet several times, switched to one foot for a while, then back to two, for a total of ten or so beautiful jumps. Then she voluntarily jumped out.

The other girls jumped in, skipped well, hopped out. It was the boys' turn. Stan jumped in too soon and the girls told him happily he was o-u-t, *out.*

"That was just practice," he retorted and went back to try again. This time he jumped in accurately and continued to do well, hopping only a few inches off the floor, just enough to clear the rope. After only a few jumps, however, he became self-conscious and jumped out. Brent, who was next, decided he didn't want to jump and Donald, behind him, also shook his head. But Richard kept it going. He had no trouble timing his entry and after a few jumps, grandstanded a little by clapping his hands at the top of each jump. No doubt he wanted to show up the girls at their own game.

The second time she jumped in, Margie didn't jump at random. She had caught the spirit of the thing and made an effort to wait for the rope. If you could judge by the way she rolled her eyes when she jumped out, she was very pleased with the way she had "solved" the rope. Stacey, the second time in, had also learned to wait for the rope. She made several graceful jumps on two feet, then several on one. I didn't believe Sandy would go again, but she did, and managed to jump twice at the right moment. She too looked happy with herself, but turned away to hide it.

I relieved the turners from duty, to give them a chance to jump. I also wanted to give some of the jumpers a turn at being the source of the rhythm of the rope. It was surprising how quickly at this point each succeeding set of rope-turners worked out a rhythm with one another. After only a few moments of working together, a rapport seemed to spring up between their respective wrist and arm muscles. Some turners, when they had a good jumper, turned with greater and greater speed each succeeding round, to force the jumper to increase his pace or miss. Some of the jumpers solved this accelerating whip of the rope so well, and loved the feeling so much, that they continued jumping until I waved them out.

I had never tried this kind of activity before, and had no idea how it would turn out. My general purpose was to let the children demonstrate to themselves their ability to create a game without props or any materials at all. I hoped thereby to demonstrate to them the power of imagination to direct action and movement. I also wanted to help them discover something of the nature of rhythm itself, by having them generate as a group a single beat they could all feel and respond to.

I stepped out of the activity altogether after they were well into it, to see if it would run by itself. It did. Their eyes and limbs and entire bodies were concentrated on the central action. Each fed it by giving himself over to the spell of the beat. They had created a magic rope and wanted to obey it. It had more power to involve and excite them than any real rope could have. The beauty I experienced watching them came from more than seeing young bodies jump and turn in a disciplined freedom of movement. The rope-jumping had tapped a kind of unconscious group energy, a current that seemed to run through them all. It had created a unity of movement that was greater than the sum of its parts. They had generated a kind of essence of rope-jumping. And, from the quiet pleasure and sense of satisfaction that came from them when we had finished, I felt they had been through an experience that had not only been fun for them, but that had moved them in a new way.

Later in the session, we tried a pantomime game of baseball. This was undertaken partly to satisfy the boys and partly to determine if a team activity would yield the same good results in group involvement as the rope-jumping had. It didn't.

For one thing, everyone wanted to bat, and everyone who batted wanted to clout a homer, nothing less. Fielders were recruited with great difficulty and only through promises of being at bat very soon. My worst mistake was in letting Donald pitch. I thought the shy towhead who had cried at Carrie's growling might profit from the pivotal role, the player who serves up the ball and controls the action. It was a case of power not corrupting, but frightening absolutely. First, Donald simply froze with the imaginary ball. When he did pitch, everyone hit homers. The second home-run hitter razzed Donald as he trotted home. Again he froze, and I gently encouraged him to try to strike out the next batter. Whereupon he began to cry. His sister and I both tried to comfort him, but it was too much for him. For me, too, and I ended the session early.

After the session, however, Nancy told me something that made me feel better. While the ball game had been in progress, some of the rope jumpers were supposed to continue practicing, so as to give this activity in front of the rest of the group the following session. Nancy had been watching and listening to these girls without letting them be aware she was doing so. She told me they had grown bored with practicing jumping and had cast about for something else to do. One said, let's play High Water Low Water. This is a game, Nancy told me, in which two players stretch a rope taut between them, and the other players have to jump over it. The rope goes higher each turn until only one player is left who can jump over it successfully. Then the process is reversed; the rope goes lower and lower until only one person is left who can go under it without touching.

They also played Snake. One person snakes the rope along the ground and everyone must hop over it. If the Snake touches you, you're out.

Since I had not seen them play, I tried to imagine how these games had worked out. In our rope-jumping, a jumper either cleared the rope or he didn't. With High Water Low Water, the invisible rope could probably also be divined by sighting from the fists of those who held the rope. But with Snake, each player was on her own recognizance, so to speak. Only each child's particular sense of scary fun could decide whether the dreaded Snake had slithered over her foot or not.

In any case, these games demonstrated for me something many others have observed: namely, that once you give children something that really interests them, an idea that kindles their imagination, they are likely to take off with it on their own. Once they are really into an idea, it is unnecessary to suggest the next thing to do, and the next. These children could easily have found an object to play hopscotch with, or played tag, or simply sat around gossiping or doing nothing. But they had discovered that playing a game without props gave them a feeling they liked, and they had extended the idea on their own to other games they knew.

Both the games they played were rope games. It was almost as if, once they had made up a rope, they had to find other ways to use it. You might call it an example of the conservation of magic.

4/ "WHO AM I?"

Carrie didn't skip rope. In fact, she was aggressively against the whole idea. When her nimble friend Lucy came near her, practicing her jumping in preparation for her turn, Carrie had laughed scornfully at her and pushed her. I guessed that this "tough" black girl who was big for her age had become so frightened of being shown up as awkward in the skipping game, she had to intimidate someone else to relieve her feelings.

I had seen real potential in Carrie. In Simon Says, she had changed from a threatening mastiff to a graceful ballet dancer. In the shopping she had done for the party, she had quickly learned to make her gestures exactly communicate her activity. I thought her decision to buy tuna over caviar was witty, and showed good judgment too. So I was eager for her to continue with the group.

However, she had also been a disruptive influence. From the first, she had bullied some of the children in various ways. Now, with the skipping incident, I had to tell her she could not continue in the group if she kept up such behavior. I had made the mistake in a previous workshop of not drawing the line firmly enough when such incidents took place. I had learned too late that two children who had dropped out of the group had done so because they had been victimized by another child.

I gave Carrie her warning gently but firmly. She reacted sullenly and I doubted that she would be back the following week.

But she did come back. There was something she wanted from the group, something important enough to her to overcome her pride. When she performed that day, I learned what it was.

The children were doing charades on the subject "Who am I?" Each was to select someone or something he wanted to portray, rehearse it by himself, or with someone else if the pantomime required two people, then give it before the group. When the charade was finished, the group would try to guess it, and the correct guesser would tell how he knew what it was.

When it was Carrie's turn, she took the stage eagerly and with surprising confidence. First, she set up an imaginary easel. Then she mixed paints, taking her time to get just the colors she wanted. She created a brush with a gesture of her hand, holding it lightly but firmly. She studied her subject (her friend Lucy was sitting for her) and painted with small, delicate strokes, controlling her movements so that she never went beyond the limits of her canvas. Carrie's actual brushwork suggested scribbling rather than painting, but the concentration in her face and the purposeful set of her whole body gripped everyone there.

For the first time that day, there was complete silence in the small gym.

As Carrie pretended to paint her friend's portrait, she was also creating a new portrait of herself for us. The media were her gestures, movements, posture and facial expressions. I had seen hints of this portrait before, in the ballet dancer and the meticulous shopper, but here it was full-blown. It was a portrait of a person — sensitive, purposeful, graceful — so unlike the manifest Carrie — bullying, sullen, awkward — as to make me believe no one, or very few, had ever seen it before.

This was no merely theatrical transformation. Nor is it important in this context whether or not Carrie has any drawing talent or aspires to become an artist. What is important is that she had chosen to show us such a portrait at all. She could have portrayed a gangster or a monster or some other all-powerful bully. That would have been safer, protecting the personality role she had chosen in "real life" and increasing her prestige as a powerful figure in the group. But the unthreatening atmosphere of the group apparently had given her the go-ahead instead to try on a secret, little-used part of herself and share it with others. She had seen a chance, so to speak, to cast herself against type, and she had seized it.

By playing the role of an artist, she was making the soft, sensitive part of herself more real to herself. As we saw with Brent on the tightrope, playing this role helped Carrie identify more closely with qualities she usually kept hidden. Her obvious involvement in the artist's role, the naturalness and confidence with which she performed it, demonstrated how central such an image was to her inner sense of herself, or rather of the self she wanted to be. The workshop was an opportunity to feed and strengthen that self.

28

There is little in Carrie's everyday world — the world of the ghetto — that does this. Most of her energy is spent trying to survive educationally, economically, socially and emotionally. Given this atmosphere, and adding the problem of her growing too fast, it is not difficult to understand why she has assumed the tough, aggressive role she plays. She is a living illustration of that old misunderstanding that the best defense is offense.

It is especially vital to help a child like Carrie to keep in touch with her inner sensitivity, and to strengthen her sense that this is a valuable part of herself. That is the function of dramatic play, with its opportunity to try out many different roles, its power to help children believe there is more in them than they can let the world see, its quality of "time out from real life."

The children spontaneously applauded when Carrie had finished her charade. It was not her performance they were applauding, but how she made them feel. For one thing, they felt relieved. They knew Carrie better now; no longer was she only someone to be afraid of. They also felt the exhilaration of new knowledge: they sensed that Carrie had revealed a part of herself the world seldom saw. Perhaps her performance made some of them more comfortable in the workshop, and encouraged them to reveal more of themselves than they intended.

They could identify with this Carrie, and admire her. Carrie's startled smile and proud fluster when she heard their applause showed that she too admired and could identify more with the Carrie just revealed. She could answer the question "Who am I?" more comprehensively and proudly than before.

5/ THE FROG AND THE CLOWN

For his charade, Stan chose something quite different. He crouched down on his haunches, leaped up, came down again. He did this twice more. At the apex of his fourth hop, he lifted his face and thrust out his tongue. He paused, then repeated the cycle several times, around and around the stage — leap, land; leap, land; leap, land; leap, lick, land; pause.

To me, it was an awesome transformation, this change of domesticated boy into wild amphibian, the more remarkable because of the nature of the boy who did it.

I glanced at the children as Stan hopped. They were as fascinated as I was. Although everyone was supposed to wait until the performer had finished before guessing at the subject, Joyce couldn't restrain a loud, impressed whisper, "It's a frog!"

"It couldn't be anything else but!" I exclaimed. I was full of enthusiasm for the frog.

"Yeah," said Margie, "but who was he sticking out his tongue at? Like this." She imitated Stan and the others giggled.

"I was catchin' flies to eat!" Stan retorted. He hadn't liked the imitation.

"Yee-uch!" said Margie. "I didn't know anyone ate flies."

"Frogs do!" said Stan.

I asked, "How many of you have ever seen a real frog?" Fewer than half the hands went up.

"Stan, why don't you tell us about frogs."

He shrugged. "They're just frogs." He looked away from me with a defensive half smile that hid anything he might be thinking. The frog had completely disappeared and he was a boy again, being asked questions.

I tried again. "We can tell you like frogs by the great way you do one. But I'd like to know *why* you like them."

Another shrug. "I just like 'em."

I gave up. It was Saturday morning after all, not a school day. "Well, that's a good enough reason," I said.

And, of course, as soon as I stopped pressing him, his own desire to share with others what he knew and felt came to the fore.

"I like 'em, well, because everyone thinks they'll feel slimy, but when you catch 'em, they just feel sticky. I like to catch 'em to show my friends, and then I let 'em go. I like to watch 'em hop away."

"Let's all be frogs," I said. The small gym was suddenly a pond full of giant frogs, hopping and licking up for insects. After a few moments, I stopped them.

"All you frogs are forgetting something. Watch the first frog again. Stan, do it again for us." He did.

"I know!" said Stacey. "He doesn't just keep hopping and hopping. He stops a minute sometimes."

"Maybe he's got to rest for the next jump," said Sally.

"Maybe," I said. "Let's all be real frogs now."

Stan was a school friend of my son Richard. Richard had wanted to come to the workshop and had invited Stan to go with him. Stan had agreed because, I assumed, he simply wanted to be with Richard. They had recently decided they were "buddies," and wanted to do everything together.

Stan had lived all his life in the suburbs. His father was a carpenter, hardworking and proud of his family and home, without many interests outside them. Stan's mother was a kind, conscientious woman, who encouraged her children without pushing them. An older daughter was in college and Stan's brother had aspirations to be a writer.

Stan himself was a polite, unexpressive and orderly boy, with a hiding-out quality about him. He seemed only to want to get by in life. His father considered him lazy at his studies. His mother helped him with his homework as often as she could. But though the emphasis at home and in school was on good grades and good behavior, Stan achieved neither. He had been put back a grade last year. And he was often caught fighting with other boys. Some of them habitually called him bad names and he tangled with them, often ending up in the principal's office. Yet Richard told me that Stan was the only boy in science class who could solve a really tough problem. And I also learned from Richard of Stan's great love and knowledge of animals.

I felt that Stan was just the kind of child who needed the expressive outlet that the workshop could provide. But though I had hopes for him, I had no idea how he would respond. For one thing, he had had little contact with city children, almost none with black children. And since his manner was to lie low and rarely express his feelings, I did not know if he would really let himself get involved in what we were doing.

As it turned out, although Stan stuck pretty close to his buddy Richard at first, his contacts with the other children, black and white, seemed natural and accepting ones. As to the lying low, the high-hopping frog was at least part of my answer.

A few Saturdays after the hopping of Stan's frog, Richard came down with a cold and could not go to the workshop with me. He called Stan to tell him, assuming, as I did, that Stan would not want to go without him. But instead, Stan said to him, "Do you think it would be all right if I came by myself?"

I was pleased and a little surprised, not only because he was willing to go without his buddy, but because he was implicitly committing himself to something he didn't have to do. After all, Saturday mornings are very good for frog-hunting. His desire to go without Richard reminded me of Carrie's returning to the workshop despite her injured pride. Clearly there was something in the workshop that he wanted.

The morning he came without Richard, Stan played tag before the session with Robin. Since the group that week was doing pantomimes in pairs, and neither Robin nor Stan had a partner, I suggested that the two of them work together on something.

Stan said he wanted to be a clown and Robin said she wanted to be a little sad orphan girl who laughed at the clown. Robin was a bright, tense, white girl from an economically depressed home. She was always eager to please, overeager in fact, and there was sometimes a hysterical note in her actions when we played pretend games. She and Stan retired to a corner of the gym to work out their pantomime. I had no opportunity to work with them before their turn on the stage came.

Robin entered first. Instead of being an orphan, she was pulling her mother to the circus with her, chattering all the while about all the beautiful things she was seeing.

"I'll go get us ten Cokes," she announced. She got the Cokes from a vending machine — they seemed to come out all at the same time — and brought them back to her seat. She said, "Oh, I don't really want a Coke. Momma, you drink them." And she gave them to her pretend mother.

Stan entered then and stepped onto a platform. Somewhere he had found a piece of green chalk, which he had used to make himself up. He had completely covered his nose and most of his cheeks with the chalk. The green nose and cheeks contrasted grotesquely with his white chin and forehead and sandy hair. He was an eerie-looking clown.

He had also found two small rubber balls, which he placed in the center of the stage. Then he returned to his platform. When Robin finally had stopped babbling to her mother, he came down from the platform. He bent from the waist to pick up the balls, one in each hand. Slowly and painfully, as if each weighed a hundred pounds, he lifted the balls off the floor. He brought them to his ankles, his knees, then to his thighs, with real strain showing in his shoulders and his masklike face. Suddenly he fell to the floor, not sparing himself in the fall, and lay still.

I was startled, certain that he had hurt himself. The other children giggled or whispered embarrassedly. Robin, however, stayed in her part, laughing and pointing at the fallen clown. Actually, it was more of a screech than a laugh.

After a few moments, Stan got up, a somewhat stunned look in his eyes. Without looking at anyone, he retrieved the balls from where they had bounced away, and replaced them in the same spot as before. Again he grasped the balls, and raised them slowly. Again he pretended they had a terrifying weight, which finally broke him and bore him violently to the ground. He varied it this time by turning an awkward somersault after taking his fall. Again, Robin screeched at him. When Stan raised himself this time, he looked crestfallen, as if the whole thing had been much harder than he had imagined.

I had hoped that the "act" was over, but when I saw him prepare to do it again, I came forward. I was torn between letting him do what he wanted and protecting him — and myself. I asked him what the balls were supposed to be.

"They're balls, but they're very heavy. You know."

"Are you supposed to hurt yourself when you fall?" He nodded, looking a little sheepish.

"*Are* you hurting yourself really when you fall down like that?" I asked.

Again he nodded, again with a sheepish look. "A little," he said. He meant, more than a little.

"Well, but you're a clown, aren't you? It doesn't seem very funny."

"I'm a sad clown."

"Well, OK," I said, "but even sad clowns don't work that hard. They'd never last in the circus if they did. They just pretend to fall. Now, instead of falling down on the floor like that, why don't you turn a couple of somersaults instead — as you did the second time, but without hurting yourself by really falling. OK?"

He tried it that way, but his interest was gone. He was simply doing what someone had told him to do.

Stan's clown reminded me of Andreyev's main character in *He Who Gets Slapped,* the respectable, suburban, middle-aged lawyer who becomes a clown to expiate his guilt. His "act" is to be slapped by another clown every night in the circus tent while everyone watches and laughs at his "mock" despair. Stan's act, well-framed for a junior Theater of Cruelty by Robin's lacerating shrieks, might have been called "He Who Falls Down."

I reflected that Stan's masochistic clown ran parallel to his fighting at school. Fighting with other boys and being sent to the principal's office were certainly ways to humiliate himself. No doubt his actions in both cases reflect buried guilt feelings that a therapist might help him with.

On the expressive level, however, both these actions may have shown his need to be a participant, to get involved, to feel something strong inside himself. Perhaps he sensed a certain thinness in his life. Carrie's ghetto world — with its variety of sights, smells, sounds and experiences, its fears, threats of violence and suffering, along with its savage joys and strong feelings overtly expressed — is at the opposite end of the pole to Stan's landscape. Stan lives in a safer, more serene world, and a much more homogenized one, in which propriety and conformity are chief values and both the showing of strong feelings and the expression of individualism are discouraged. Stan tries to conform to his world, but underneath he feels the need for something else. The fights at school satisfy something in him. The fighting relationship is at least a strong one; he feels something when he fights. He is also defining and asserting his individuality: "I am a boy who fights and gets sent to the principal's office — that's who I am!" He was also asserting a strong and original identity with his violent clown. In both, part of the drama is that he must be punished for his rebellion.

Then there's that perky frog. Richard had told me how Stan is always after him to help hunt frogs. Here again, Stan may be seeking something more than what he finds in his daily life. But here he goes to nature and finds a free and wild creature to identify with. In the murky greenness of the frog swamp, a part of Stan that usually lies buried can hop about. Here he can think thoughts that have no practical use or even meaning. He can dream of mysteries and possibilities that lead nowhere but further into himself. The frogs ask no questions and give him no exams. With them, he can be a creature who neither fails nor succeeds, but simply is.

Assuming that the frog and the clown are indeed important inner images to Stan, why did he choose to expose them to us? It would have been easier, and certainly more characteristic, to lie low and do something that had less emotional significance to him. The fact is, the workshop situation contained an ideal means to fulfill Stan's need to communicate himself to others. The drive to tell others who we are, how we feel, what things mean to us is timeless and almost universal. Probably it is the need to assuage our aloneness and to signal others that we need understanding and comfort. In our culture, it is difficult to do this directly, since we are so defensive and reserved in expressing our feelings. But the stage can function as a kind of screening device, an acceptable way to lay aside the public mask and show the private face.

So it functioned for Stan. Actually, I believe it was a sign of health in Stan to choose these roles to play for us, just because they were so important to him. It was also a

37

sign that Stan has much unexplored creative capacity in himself. There was crude but true art in Stan's perky frog and poignant clown; his deeper feelings inspired and penetrated the images he showed us. The workshop not only gave him the opportunity to act out these images, it also showed him how he could harness his feelings for creative endeavor. Perhaps the experience will serve him as a precedent for future growth.

6 / ciNdEREllA

The week before Halloween, I suggested to the children that they wear their trick-or-treat costumes to the next session. Brent, the ex–tightrope-walker, came as an astronaut, complete with space helmet and life-support suit. This encouraged me. Brent had played the games and done some pantomimes with others, but he was still wary of the group and stayed at its edges. And though most of the children by this time had been willing to try something alone in front of the rest of the group, Brent had not.

Once, as a kind of creative catharsis, I had asked them all to yell as loudly as they could, in unison. It was good and deafening, and they enjoyed it. Then I asked each one to yell in turn. Some of them had trouble letting go, but after some encouragement and a few tries, most of them made a noise of some sort. Brent just shook his head when his turn came.

"Let's just see what would happen, Brent," I insisted. "Come on, just try." He couldn't do it.

But now there was the astronaut costume. I assumed he identified with the hero it represented and may even have worn it to help him do what he was afraid to do before. He didn't volunteer when I asked who wanted to act out his costume and I didn't expect him to do so. I did believe that when I called on him after a few children had performed, he would be ready to do something. But I was wrong.

He shook his head when I suggested he show us his moon walk. Since he had previously been willing to work with someone else, I suggested that he pretend he was landing on the moon with a fellow astronaut. Again he shook his head.

Of course, I was disappointed, but later I felt that Brent may have taken my eagerness for him to do something alone as a kind of pressure. The same might be said of urging him to shout. John Holt says in *How Children Learn*, "If we don't push a child beyond the limits of his courage, he is sure to get braver." Actually, Brent's simple willingness to wear his costume to the workshop must have taken some courage, given his problems. Urging him to shout with all the other children watching him, or to perform by himself in front of them, may easily have been pushing him beyond the limits of his courage. The pressure, regardless of any good intentions behind it, only made him withdraw further into himself and perhaps even brought out a kind of stubborn defiance. I resolved to stop pushing Brent.

We had no stage to work on that Saturday. The church was sponsoring an art exhibit and pictures were on all the walls and strung on wires across the stage. This was an annoying surprise to me. Since we had been using the stage regularly up to now, I felt that losing it would break the continuity for the children. When they came in that morning, they looked around with some bewilderment. Several wandered up to the stage and came back to me with things like: "Hey, there's pictures all over the stage. We can't do anything today." Or: "There's no place to do anything. What are we going to do?"

There was a small platform in the middle of the gym. I pointed to it and said, "We'll use that platform. It's as good as a stage."

I said it without conviction, just to keep things going, but I turned out to be right. Once we got started, the children adapted to the restricted playing space with little problem. In fact, what they lost in freedom of movement was more than made up for by what they gained in body control. With their movements more constricted, their playing became more compact. They made fewer meaningless gestures and movements. As a matter of fact, there was a bonus for me in it: there was less "messing around" than when they had a cyclorama, curtain and wings to do it in. And I sensed a closer involvement in what was happening on the platform by those in the audience.

After that, I used the stage somewhat less. A stage is glamorous and appealing; if you have one, you use it. But we did not require it. Altogether, the experience taught me that children are prisoners of habit only if you are. And that "two boards and a passion" are indeed all you need for drama, or for a children's drama workshop!

Carrie, fresh from her triumph as The Artist, showed up in a fairy godmother costume. Obviously, she wanted to try another role of delicacy and grace. The costume included a long, sequined gown and a grinning white cardboard mask with painted golden hair. (I wondered whether she would have put on a black fairy godmother mask if she could have found one, or if fairy godmothers were only white, in her mind.)

The *pièce de résistance* of Carrie's costume was a wand whose tip lit up when a button was pressed. Everyone gathered around her to see how it worked. The wand glowed on and off like a firefly as she proudly showed it off.

Carrie and her friend Lucy played the key scene from Cinderella in pantomime. Cinderella, also in a long dress, sat in the corner of the platform, staring into space. The fairy godmother entered, her wand glowing on and off, as if giving away free samples of the magic to come. Cinderella looked up. Grinning her painted grin, the godmother got to the point without preliminaries. She touched the girl of the cinders on the shoulder with her battery-powered wand. Cinderella stood up, not altering her expression. She looked down at herself and whirled completely around. Then they both looked at me, the miracle too quickly over.

I asked the group what they had liked in the skit. Several answered to the same effect: they liked it when Cinderella had turned all about and looked at herself. Why that part? I asked.

No one answered at first. Then Stacey said, "Well, you got the idea something had happened to her."

"Yes," I said. "The fun of a story is not just what happens, but what happens to the person because of what happened in the story. Anything else they could have done to tell the story better, Stacey?"

"Well," she said, "Cinderella could have seemed more, you know, surprised."

"That's true. When a big, sudden change happens to you, you're definitely surprised. And there was certainly a big change in Cinderella. From rags to riches, you might say. From sad to happy, from plain to very beautiful. Can you think of anything you know about that does that, that changes like that?"

"Like when I get a new dress?" said Joyce.

"Yes, you and Cinderella. What else changes from ugly to pretty?"

"A chicken," said Margie.

"What about a chicken?"

"The way it looks before my mommy cooks it and when I eat it."

"Oh, right. Very good. It looks naked and raw before it goes into that oven but it's golden and delicious-looking when it comes out. Good. What about people changing like that?"

Lucy said, "My mommy and daddy change when they go out together."

"Absolutely. They look like different people and feel like it too, I'll bet. Now we're rolling. Who else has a change?"

"A tadpole changes into a frog," said Stan.

"It sure does." I smiled at Stan's pet obsession. "What else?"

"A flower," said Amy, who had a garden.

"How do you mean?"

"A flower seed becomes a flower, right?"

"Right," I said. "You know I was just reading that some people believe that plants have feelings, just like we do. Why don't we all pretend we're flower seeds. Close your eyes for a minute and think about how it feels to be a seed, sleeping in the winter earth, waiting for the spring sun. I'll be the spring sun and you all be sleeping seeds. Can we try it?"

Some of the children crouched near their chairs, covering their faces with their arms and drawing up their knees, foetuslike. Others lay full length on the floor, on their backs or stomachs. A few simply sat on their chairs, heads bowed, eyes shut tight, arms and legs rigidly crossed.

"That's fine. Okay, now, the first rains of spring have come and are almost over. There's a rainbow up here in the sky, though you can't see it yet. And here comes the sun. I'm coming out from behind the last rain clouds. I'm nice and warm — do you feel me? Feels good after all that snow and cold, doesn't it? It feels so good you begin to push down some roots. And now that you feel the sun, you want to see it. Very slowly, you start to push up through the earth. That's right, push up. Now you're getting some food and water through your roots and you feel stronger. You push harder and harder and harder — and you break through. You're a tiny green shoot just poking above the cold wet earth and you see the sun! Do you see me? I make you feel happy, don't I? You want to get closer to me, so you grow some more, and then some more. You get happier now that you see how beautiful the rainbow is, the whole world is. You raise yourself toward the sun, stretching higher and higher. You put out leaves to feel more warmth. You put out buds and, finally, the buds begin to uncurl, get bigger, open up. Then, you bloom!"

As I spoke, the "foetuses" slowly uncurled, became babies, turned into children standing on their own feet, arms raised upward. The flat prone bodies rounded themselves to a sitting position, rose up, and slowly expanded outward. The bowed heads straightened, the eyes opened, the arms uncrossed and, tentaclelike, waved and fluttered, while the legs straightened and became stems supporting the blossoming plants.

"I see a whole garden of flowers smiling up at me. It's beautiful."

Reluctantly the flowers turned into children again. As they resumed their chairs, they were smiling and pleased with themselves.

"Now, Carrie and Lucy, try your pantomime again. Think of Cinderella as a story about change. When you're young, you're changing faster than at any other time of your life. You're getting bigger, learning new things, changing your feelings and your ideas all the time. Even when you're grown, you change, and the world changes too. That's the one thing you can be sure of, that things change.

"In the old days, the most important change was the change in season, from winter to spring. You couldn't raise food in winter and if the sun didn't come back, everyone would die. We take this change for granted now, but then it seemed like magic, and people prayed to the gods to make the sun come back. They told themselves stories, too, stories about plain girls in the cinders changed by magic into beautiful princesses. They liked that story because it made them feel that change could happen, from ugly to beautiful, from cold to warm, from winter to spring.

"So, Cinderella, think of yourself first as a plain, ugly seed sleeping under the cold earth. Maybe the winter is like your stepmother and stepsisters, telling the seed that she's ugly and good for nothing but lying in the cold ground. Somewhere inside you, you feel there might be something else, something you would show everybody if you could, but you're not sure because you're just a plain seed in the ground. Then Carrie comes along and taps you with her magic wand and changes you. You don't believe it at first — how could this happen to *you*? But then, little by little, you begin to believe it. You change inside as well as outside and you show us that. Finally, finally, you bloom — into a beautiful girl with glass slippers who's ready to dance with a prince.

"And you, Fairy Godmother, you're very important. You know who you are? You're really the springtime in disguise. The tip of your magic wand lights up and you know what it is? It's the sun! Only *you* can change the seed into the flower, the plain girl in the cinders into the most beautiful girl in the kingdom. Want to try it again?"

Carrie entered, this time with deliberation. Instead of moving directly to Cinderella, she circled around her for a few moments in a slow dance, her movements expressing the dignified weight of her office. And the wand was dark until, finally, she touched Cinderella with the glowing light.

When the wand touched her, Cinderella looked up distrustfully at the fairy godmother. She looked down at herself and frowned, shaking her head in disbelief, almost disapproval. She rose from her crouch slowly, stared at the fairy godmother, then at the wand. Finally, she looked down at herself again, at her feet. There were the glass slippers. Her eyes got wide. She picked up the folds of her dress and holding them up, slowly turned about, looking down at the dress as she turned. She dropped the dress, raised both her arms outward like leaves growing from a branch. She looked out at us, and her face bloomed into a dazzling smile.

No doubt the fairy tale had lit up the girls' imaginations when they first heard it or read it. But the feeling had long since been forgotten. When they first played it for us, they presented only the surface actions of the plot, as if that were the story. The second time around was different. It was different because the characters now had a life of their own and the story had some personal meaning to the children. They connected their personal experiences and observations of change with the events of the story. By impersonating the natural transformation of seed into flower they understood on a different level the other, mythic, transformation of plain girl into princess-elect. Relating the two — the awakening of Cinderella's beauty and the awakening of a flower — gave the story an added dimension of mystery in their imaginations.

For Carrie and Lucy, playing a part in the story made the story part of them and opened them up once again to the excitement they felt when they heard the tale for the first time.

Lucy herself was something of a real-life Cinderella. This was not merely because her family had recently moved from a black ghetto to an integrated lower-middle-class housing development, and she now wore neat and pretty clothes.

When she had come to her first workshop (this was her second time around), she had been almost unable to do anything beyond what she was directed to do. In a group game, she would watch what others did and copy that. In a pantomime or improvisation, she always had to be told several times what to do, and when she started to move into it, she looked as stiff and apprehensive as if she were plunging into cold water. And the "cold water" got to her. Often, when she was in the middle of an action, just as she was gaining some momentum, she froze. She would stop short, squeeze her eyes shut in a pained self-deprecating way, and clap both hands over her mouth, as if to say, "Oh, I goofed. Now I'm going to be yelled at!" Her body seemed to go blank along with her mind.

As I got to know Lucy, I surmised that there was a lot of

47

pressure in her life — to be good, to stay still, to do what she was told. Lucy's parents clearly wanted the best for their daughter and gave her all they could. But it's quite possible that their anxiety to be accepted in their new white-dominated environment made them demand that their daughter be a model of deportment, or what they considered to be such a model. Anything spontaneous in her behavior was frowned upon; it called too much attention to herself and her family. For black children living among whites, it's best to lie low and behave. Why risk criticism? Why encourage people to talk behind your back?

At first, when Lucy froze in the middle of an action, I tried to thaw her out with encouragement to go on, to finish what she started. I soon gave that up. It doesn't help to tell a frightened child not to be frightened. The change can only take place inside, when the pressure is removed and an atmosphere that allows some freedom and spontaneity is substituted.

Slowly, Lucy began to relate the workshop activities to her private life, where no adult eyes censored her. She learned that whether she "goofed" in a role or simply did nothing, no one was going to yell at her. The internal critic, which was so sharp with her when she made a mistake or forgot what to do, lost a little of its power. In the games and pantomimes, she began to do things that came out of her imagination. A pixie quality began to emerge, too. She would never permit herself to misbehave or be wild in any way, but sometimes I could see some merry mischief in her eyes and actions. She came to feel much easier doing things in front of the group. In fact, her personality seemed to expand and flower in the attention the group gave her. She still spoke too softly to be heard much of the time and the self-critical crinkling of her eyes in the middle of an action sometimes appeared. But the freezing and guilty clapping of her hands over her mouth stopped completely. In fact, the day I asked each of them to yell, a small but very respectable cry came out of her.

One day, Lucy made up and organized a skit with several of her friends. She played a first-grade teacher and her friends played students. First, she gave them reading lessons. They were supposed to be beginning readers and read haltingly. Actually, the children were making up the primer as they went along. When a child mispronounced a word, Lucy corrected her gently.

She sent a child to the blackboard to do a problem.

"You know how to do this, don't you?" she asked encouragingly.

The child said she did. But she did it wrong and Lucy corrected her mistake. The child did another one, correctly this time, and Lucy praised her. Another child had forgotten her homework.

"Children shouldn't forget their homework," Lucy said in quiet admonition. She let the child go home to get it.

A girl entered. "There's a new girl today," said Lucy, taking her hand. "Her name is Rose Ann. Will you please help her if she gets stuck." Each of the children said hello to the new girl and shook her hand.

This was a first for Lucy: the first time she had been given the chance to objectify — she created it, organized it, and cast it — a fantasy that was important to her. For once, she could be the wielder of power and authority, instead of being their object. And the touching thing about it was the way she wielded that power and authority. It was the opposite of a fantasy of revenge, of I'm top dog now, so watch out! Instead, she was the very model of a teacher, firm and in control but sympathetic to the needs and problems of her charges. Naturally, she was somewhat biased toward the child's point of view in playing the teacher's role. But the point is that she was acting out what she would like adults to be, how she herself wanted to be treated by them. The girl who forgot her homework, the slow reader, the girl who made a mistake at the blackboard, the new girl — each showed a facet of Lucy's own fears, and to each, Lucy the teacher applied reassurance and sympathy.

When the skit was over and the children were about to take their seats again, I saw Lucy clap her hands over her mouth. That again, I thought.

"Something wrong, Lucy?"

"We forgot something. Can we do it now. Please."

I said they could. Actually, I was very happy that Lucy was asserting herself, in her modest way. Here's what Lucy wanted to say to complete her fantasy skit:

"Children, today is half a day of school. Tomorrow, there's no school, so you can stay home. The next day is Wednesday and now I want to give you a note for your parents, so they'll come Wednesday and see what you're doing here. So take your books now and go play the rest of the day. Okay?"

Pressures on Lucy will continue at home and in the world. But at least there was a place where her pixie got loose a little. A place she could shape a world she would like to live in. A place where she could be Cinderella, a girl at first forced to follow a strict code of behavior but then transformed into someone who could become what was in her to become.

Perhaps the playing of such roles was a step in "becoming" for Lucy. After all, the important change in Cinderella was not her beautiful new gown but the new feeling about herself that took place inside.

7/ witch's soup

Margie, the impish nine-year-old, was ready to do her Halloween pantomime. She wore no costume: she was much too independent a girl to wear a costume just because others did.

Everyone sat forward a little. Something interesting usually happened when Margie performed. You could never predict her. She had a cool, cocky, self-absorbed way of doing things that lent special conviction to her performance and made her fun to watch.

First, she pantomimed a long, enigmatic telephone conversation with someone. She ranged about with the phone receiver, listening with great concentration, registering respect and even awe for the person on the other end of the wire. Yet there was a slight smile on her face as well, which parodied her seriousness. Once she raised her eyebrows in surprise. She wrote something down and laughed silently at what she had written.

She hung up finally and began to pantomime some elaborate cooking preparations. She opened drawers and reached up to shelves, getting out all manner of bowls and beaters, spoons and sifters. She opened a refrigerator, looked in appraisingly, and began taking out various objects. Then she crossed the stage, stood on her tiptoes, and took down a huge, heavy container, which she created with wide open arms and a stagger or two as she carried it over to her stove.

She lit a fire. Into the massive pot she began to drop a series of ingredients. She cracked an imaginary egg into the pot. Then she appeared to throw in the eggshells too! She put in something round, something square and something long and thin, which she held up fastidiously by one end before letting the pot claim it. She uncorked a small bottle, smelled it, wrinkled her nose, and poured in the contents, to the last drop. With a casual air, she let the bottle fall in too. Sometimes, as with the egg or the bottle, you could easily recognize the exact object; sometimes not. But you could always surmise each item's size and weight. Her mien was serious and preoccupied throughout; as far as one could tell, the audience didn't exist for her. Never once did she hesitate before making her next move. It was not as if she had rehearsed it all beforehand, but that she kept her objective firmly in mind at all times, and let nothing distract her.

She stirred, tasted, and reflected a moment. Then she crossed to the other side of the stage again for more ingredients. I had asked the children to keep their pantomimes reasonably brief, so we could get around to everyone. Margie, however, had long since passed her limit and showed no signs of finishing. She loved to be onstage and I hated to stop her, but I finally had to. I asked the group for guesses about what she had been doing.

Everyone knew she had been cooking something, but they had many versions as to what it was. Someone said she was making a birthday cake for a giant. Another, a crazy stew. A third, making breakfast for a big monster family. A boy said she wasn't making anything, just fooling around up there. The child who had performed was supposed to stay up front to field the guesses. Characteristically, Margie had ignored this and gone straight back to her seat. She had brought a bright-colored piece of wool with her and was soon busy making knots in it. She made her knots, meanwhile shaking her head no to all the guesses.

"All right," I said. "We give up. Tell us what you were making."

"Witch's soup," she said, her voice muffled as she bent to tie a big knot.

"Witch's brew?" I asked.

"Witch's soup!" she insisted. "Soo-oup!"

"Oh." I said.

"Ohhh!" said everyone, nodding heads. The pantomime had been long and a little repetitious, but now it seemed worth it.

"That's a very good idea, Margie," I said. "What was that phone call at the beginning?"

"The witch was telling me what she wanted in it."

"And what did she want in it?"

"Some yucky pills. Rotten eggs and eggshells. A big long mouse. And poison, a lot of poison. Rat poison. I forget the other things."

"Those are very good things for witch's soup," I said.

"Do you mind if we put in some more things?" Margie shook her head; no, she didn't mind. She was busy with her knots.

"Who's got something they want to put into Margie's witch's soup?"

"A skunk," someone said.

"Rusty nails. A lot of rusty nails and some garbage."

"A girl's head," said a boy.

"A boy's head," retorted a girl. "And his hands and dirty feet too!"

"The dirt under my fingernails."

"Marijuana."

"A slimy snake, and a lot of slimy baby snakes."

"Iodine!"

"Spinach!"

"My constipation pills."

"My report card!"

"Right . . . great . . . terrific!" I exclaimed, delighted at how many of them were throwing in ideas, even those who rarely spoke up. Like Falstaff, Margie was not only witty in herself, she was the cause of wit in others. Costume or not, she had certainly contributed to the spirit of the holiday. She had made the creative leap from a garden-variety, broom-riding, cackling Halloween witch to a cool, handy, imaginative witch's cook. It was a good example of how a child will come up with an original idea — her own kind of idea — when given the freedom to do so. It was also a good instance of how other children can get involved in an idea that intrigues them, building on it with thoughts of their own; Margie had stimulated a Halloween brainstorming session!

Margie, like Lucy, was a second-timer in the workshop. It had been a long way from the Lucy who froze in the middle of an action to the Lucy who could sustain five minutes of playing a first-grade teacher. It had been an equally long way from the Margie of early workshop sessions to the girl who could create and play a straight-faced, well-controlled witch's soupmaker.

The way each had traveled to arrive at her respective achievement in the workshop was quite different, because their starting points had been different. Where Lucy was inhibited, Margie was a show-off. Where Lucy was reluctant to do anything, Margie wanted to do everything. Where Lucy did only what she was told, Margie wanted to do only what she pleased. Since their problems and personalities varied, their needs did too. Lucy needed encouragement to get over her self-consciousness and an environment to help her gain the courage to overcome her fear of failure; Margie needed something quite different. When she began in the workshop, Margie's energy and her drive to dramatize herself were leaking away in frantic attempts to gain attention. Her need was certainly not for repressive outside control, to "make her behave herself," but for motivation to develop more self-control. She had to learn that disciplining herself had rewards of its own. It is a striking fact that the kind of activity I am describing can help meet the needs of both a Lucy and a Margie.

It was clear to me early in the workshop that Margie was likely to be a problem child. For one thing, she made comments while other children were in the middle of their pantomimes. The comments were often amusing, but naturally had a disruptive effect. When she wasn't making remarks, Margie often decided she had to go to the bathroom or get a drink of water in the middle of someone's work. She wore taps on her shoes and would go clicking across the floor, heedless of the commotion she was causing.

She would be the first to volunteer for any role, but more often than not, when she got onstage, she would find an excuse to run into the wings and hide, or wrap herself in the cyclorama until unraveled. When she did settle down and decide to do something in front of the group, she played it "strictly for laughs," making jokes or mugging, without much attempt to communicate anything but her love of the spotlight. At these times her talent for entertaining was clearly in evidence; so was her lack of self-discipline.

Her other mode was pouting. When I spoke to her in exasperation, asking her to stay in her seat or to be quiet while others were working, she would look at me reproachfully and begin to suck her thumb. Her eyes would glaze over and she would be completely passive the rest of that session.

Reluctantly, I began to feel that Margie was not yet ready for such a group. I couldn't seem to find a way to help her move beyond the silly show-off stage, and her behavior was beginning to infect the other children and make work difficult.

Once, when she was being especially troublesome, she looked over at me with her impish brown eyes and said, "Margie's really naughty, isn't she?"

"Is that what your mother says when you do this at home?"

She nodded. "My teacher, too."

"Why do you think you do it?"

She squeezed her eyes shut in a self-critical grimace, shook her head rapidly back and forth, and said, "Because . . . I'm . . . naughty!"

"Well, Margie, I don't think you're naughty. But I do think everyone has a right to his turn and that's impossible if it's always Margie's turn."

Finally, through an act of mine that did not have her welfare as its object at all, Margie began to benefit from the workshop. Two of the mothers who brought children to the workshop — one was Margie's mother — had younger children as well, both six-year-old girls. Because of home circumstances, they had to bring the younger ones along with them when they brought the older ones. Since they lived a distance away and would have to entertain the younger children for an hour and a half while the older ones were attending our sessions, they asked if the former could sit in too, on a trial basis.

I doubted it would work, but agreed. After a trial period, I found the younger children could not sustain the interest and attention needed. I asked their mothers to make other arrangements now and enroll the small ones the following year or so. It was in this way that Kitty, Margie's younger sister, was withdrawn from the group.

With the departure of her little sister, a change became perceptible in Margie. Where before she had stayed near her sister, she now began to make friends with the two older girls in the workshop, Amy and Sally. She began to copy their more restrained behavior. She continued to find it hard to sit still while others were doing something, but she didn't interrupt so often or noisily tap out to the drinking fountain. She sucked her thumb much less and participated more often.

Of course I speculated on the reasons for the change and of course, though I knew little more about the family situation than what I saw, I drew some conclusions. I thought that perhaps Margie had been reproducing a home rivalry at the workshop. When the new child came home from the hospital, perhaps Margie was not prepared for the big change in her life which would ensue. A glutton for attention as it was, she must have been frantic to see so much of the attention she regarded as her divine right shift to the new arrival. Somehow she had to get that spotlight back for herself. She seized on two related ways to do so: she "acted silly" to get everyone to look at her and not her rival. And she reverted to her own babyhood behavior on the reasonable assumption: "If babies get so much attention, I'll be a baby again."

Since in reality she was no longer a baby but a "big girl" she felt guilty about her actions. When exasperated adults called her "naughty," she agreed with them, at least partly. Perhaps they punished her, and that made her "act up" all the more; they were paying attention to her, weren't they? And so a destructive cycle gained momentum, one of the worst parts of which was this: Margie was learning to condemn her own self-expressiveness because it coincided with behavior stigmatized as "naughty." In the workshop, Margie was compelled to devote her energies to distracting attention from her rival.

So ran my speculations, based on the classic sibling rivalry syndrome. For all of this, however, the departure of her little sister was no more than a catalyst for Margie's progress. The more important factor was that the workshop itself offered Margie a chance for growth. Children often ask for "one more chance" when they misbehave or "act up"; I'm sure Margie did this often. But if the atmosphere a child lives in is nonaccepting, the new chance is not really new. The child has a built-in set of reactions to that atmosphere, and the same behavior will usually reoccur. But an accepting atmosphere that encouraged expressiveness, such as the workshop's, held out a truly new chance for Margie. With her sister gone, she could respond to it.

From the beginning, I had let Margie do almost as she

pleased when she performed before the group. I felt that her mugging and cracking jokes, though far from creative dramatics, was at least an outlet for her drive to entertain. I also felt that if she got a taste of being admired for "acting up" rather than always being criticized or even punished for it, she could retain some feeling that her self-expressive part was valuable, rather than "naughty."

She did get satisfaction from the other children's appreciation of her antics. When her sister left and her compulsion merely to show off lessened, she began to feel the satisfactions of performing, for their own sake. She began to seek more of those satisfactions.

I believe it began to dawn on her at this point that this was a place where you were *supposed* to show off and that there were people who enjoyed seeing you do it. You weren't naughty at all when you did it there. She lost little of her "cock of the walk" manner, but she stopped a great deal of her random mugging and silliness. Creating a character or playing out a fantasy of her own became a serious business to her. The motivation was the same as before, the need for attention and approval, but now she had a reason to discipline herself: she had discovered that the *quality* of the attention she received had improved. People not only paid attention to her but admired her when she exercised some inner control of herself and channeled her energy and imagination into some creative shape, such as making a witch's soup.

This had an effect on her offstage behavior too. It was as if her newfound status as performer no longer fit with her old role as disturber of the peace. She took on a certain dignity; actually this was natural with her — it was only a matter of letting it come through. And this dignity was reinforced by her identification with the older girls who were now her friends. Also, she was probably concerned that the group might deny her their attention and applause if she remained a "babyish" figure.

Margie's progress was made manifest during a long, complicated improvisation created and staged by her two older friends, Amy and Sally. Amy played the famous detective Sherlock Holmes and Sally, the detective's boss. A murder had been committed. Clues were scattered all over the world. There was a plot against Sherlock's life, and many sinister characters lurked about. While Amy and Sally stayed in their own roles throughout, Margie played everybody else. She was a nasty child. (She played that role on her knees, but didn't suck her thumb.) She was a spy for a rival detective. She was a spooky butler. And she was a wicked rich lady who fired a bow and arrow at Sherlock because he was about to discover that she was the murderess.

I would have guessed that Margie felt overjoyed that the older girls trusted her to such an extent in their improvisation but nothing in her self-possessed manner betrayed it. A certain Margie-like tone ran through all her roles — a wackiness mixed with a cool "I don't care" hauteur — but she carried every part through and was on time for every entrance and exit. She even successfully played in a scene with Sherlock and the boss which required her to be a completely silent and attentive listener. To me, that was more of a mystery than the one onstage; I shook my head a little in disbelief.

Something else was noticeable during the improvisation: we could understand most of what Margie was saying. She had always slurred her speech somewhat, so that I would often ask her to repeat what she was saying; nor would the repetition be much of an improvement. Once, after a session, her mother had told me that Margie had always had trouble in this area. It was as if she were always talking to herself, her mother said, not to others. The school had suggested she be given a speech tutor, and the tutor had worked hard having Margie pronounce sounds, syllables and words over and over. It had not helped.

After the Sherlock Holmes session was over, I mentioned Margie's improvement in speaking to her mother. She told me that she, and Margie's teacher as well, had noticed definite progress in her ability to speak clearly since Margie had been attending the workshop.

It was not too difficult to figure out why this was happening. Certainly it was not due to my nagging Margie that we couldn't understand her. But my reminders did make her aware that she wasn't getting across to her audience. Margie now had a real ego stake in the workshop. She was getting great satisfaction out of creating and performing for us. Therefore she had a strong inner motivation to speak more clearly: what good is it to say something funny that you've made up, or something important to a story you're acting out, if no one understands you? She no longer could just "talk to herself"; she had an audience out there listening to what she was saying, and she wanted very much for them to understand her.

Out of this incentive, the new habit of speaking clearly began slowly to displace the old habit of slurring her speech. She began to speak more clearly offstage too. As everyone knows who has tried to change a habit, it takes a powerful motivation to do so. Apparently, Margie had that motivation.

John Holt has noted in *How Children Learn*, "Children have their own need to learn and resist learning what they have no need for." Making Margie, especially Margie, pronounce sounds and words over and over to improve her speech was just the way to arouse her resistance. A dog will retrieve a stick over and over because it's a game for him and he is praised for playing it. But rote repetition for a child, though it has been an educational method for centuries, certainly seems in many cases to be the hard way to teach, and learn. There is little incentive for a child in such learning, little that arouses his own need to learn.

It would seem, too, that often the best learning takes place when the child does not know, nor is made to realize, that he is being taught. This is certainly true for an independent-minded girl like Margie. I did not say to her, "I want you to learn to speak more clearly." I said, "Your audience cannot understand what you're saying." She didn't like to hear either statement, but the latter was aimed to activate her own motivation, her own need to learn, not to press the claim of a teacher.

The need of a Margie for attention is perhaps outsized. But few children receive the attention or the respect they need to feel valuable and important. A friend once told me of the tension she felt when as a child she prepared for her semiannual piano recital for parents and friends. But tense as she was, she looks back upon those recitals with satisfaction, because they were among the few occasions when adults viewed her with undivided attention and with respect.

In our workshop, children received the attention and respect of their peers, and of their director too, of course. This fills an important need. It also can provide a powerful thrust for inner development, as we have seen in Margie's case. Margie's first progress in the group was her improving ability to control her wayward impulses. Then, as her motivation increased — caused by the growing desire to be recognized and applauded for what she created — her development accelerated. Margie moved from checking her impulse to wrap herself in a cyclorama to becoming a witty witch's cook to being able to speak more clearly. The workshop had nourished Margie well by stirring the magic ingredients of creative theater into the "soup" of her inner life.

8 / THE SAd bRidE

Lucy (Cinderella) helped her friend Joyce do a pantomime that Joyce had made up. (Joyce was the girl who
wanted Stan and Richard to paint a real table rather than
an imaginary one.) Both Joyce and Lucy were in long
dresses and did their skit around the platform. They were
both brides and came down the aisle together, as if they
were marrying each other, or as if this were a wedding
ceremony for brides only.

They walked very slowly, in wedding-march fashion,
side by side, each holding an imaginary bouquet of flowers, their eyes demurely cast down. They marched once
around the platform, mounted it together at the back,
walked three steps across its surface, and stopped at the
edge. Lucy raised her eyes and smiled at the audience,
then pantomimed tossing her bouquet at us — the old

custom of throwing out the hope of a husband to the other girls. She flung it in a wide arc with a big gesture. Sally rose up and pretended to catch it. Everyone enjoyed that and our eyes went to Joyce, awaiting the toss of her bouquet as well.

Joyce stood in the same position, her eyes still downcast, her usual fixed half smile on her face. A few moments passed. The unfinished ceremony stood in limbo as we waited. Finally, she released her flowers. But instead of flinging them away, she gave them a little rueful push, and remained transfixed, staring at the place the flowers would have fallen.

I said, "Well, Joyce, that was good, but when you've just been married and throw your bouquet away for the other girls to catch, how do you feel? Aren't you happy?" She shook her head no.

"Oh, you're not a happy bride, is that it?" She nodded. "Don't you like the man you married?" No answer. "Or maybe he didn't show up?" Same nonresponse, same fixed smile. "Well, it doesn't matter. If you're a sad bride, that's just the way you'd throw your bouquet. But you know, we weren't sure because you seemed to be smiling a little bit. Try it again, but this time show us how you feel with your face and eyes. Then toss your flowers away."

Joyce shook her head; no, she didn't want to do it again. She didn't need to. Her face was now quite serious. I thought she was going to cry. She didn't, but went back to her seat and turned her back to us.

"You know," I said, "Joyce is right. We think all brides are happy, but I'm sure there's the other kind too — the sad bride. Lucy was the happy bride and Joyce was the unhappy bride. It was a good idea to show us both kinds."

While the next child did his skit, I sat next to Joyce and asked in a whisper what was wrong. She had her eyes closed and shook her head. Obviously, she had not merely been acting out an idea, but had expressed in a disguised way something she was feeling deeply. The sad bride had a meaning, as a dream has a meaning. I didn't know what it was and she wouldn't tell me.

Since I first met Joyce, I had been especially moved by her. There was a special integrity of feeling in the things she did. She was moody, often unresponsive, even contrary and stubborn at times, but there was a glow about her that arose not only from intelligence and alertness but even more from a quality of seeming to respond only to inner demands. She was always herself.

She had an original way of looking at the world which was naïve and knowing at the same time. Her idea that Stan and Richard should have used a real table was primitive in a sense, but it cut to the heart of a real question. Once, in her soft-voiced, reticent way, she had raised her hand and guessed someone's pantomime. I asked her to come up front and tell us about it in detail. She made her usual face, but came. She stood fidgeting for a moment, not looking at us, and then she began to pantomime describing the other child's pantomime. She pretended to explain, using elaborate gestures and facial expressions, but no words came out.

I doubt if it was her intention to parody the conventions of the group, even though that was the effect. She was up front, so she felt she had to do something. The customary response didn't appeal to her at that moment, or perhaps she felt too shy to talk. Another child might have forced himself to stammer something or pouted or simply been paralyzed, but not Joyce. Something of her own bubbled up in her to do, so she did it.

I may have been the only one who enjoyed Joyce's unconscious little satire. The other children had Joyce down in their book as a bit "queer" and probably looked upon her impromptu explanation pantomime as only another manifestation of her strangeness. Joyce had friends in the group but mainly her status was a set-apart one. Sometimes, she literally set herself apart. During the sessions when we used the stage, the group sat in informal rows on folding chairs a few feet from the stage. Joyce, however, would place her chair right at the foot of the low stage wall. She would lean her elbow on the stage apron itself and gaze up at the players as they performed. It was as if she lived in all the fantasies that moved about the stage and wanted to be as close to them as possible.

Once she kept her coat on (she had a maxi which covered her completely) when the session began. She had done this before, but had removed the coat, reluctantly, when I suggested it. This particular day she shook her head when I said, "It's pretty warm in here, Joyce. Why not take off your coat?"

I felt she had her reasons and didn't insist. Later, she got involved in a pantomime with two other children. When they were due to perform it, I casually said she would be able to move around more freely without her coat. She took it off without a murmur and revealed a very pretty green dress as she ran up to the stage.

The coat business puzzled me. I asked Margie privately during our break why she thought Joyce had wanted to keep her coat on.

Margie said simply, "We're all wearing pants."

Pure male blindness! I should have seen it as soon as Joyce took her coat off. Girls especially are sensitive to being dressed differently than everyone else. Still, it seemed on further reflection to be an overreaction. And actually Joyce stood out even more wearing a coat when no one else did. What I learned later about Joyce's special situation in life threw light on the coat incident along with much else. It only went to show again that one must know the basic facts about children's lives to have any understanding of why they do what they do.

Very small children are radicals of feeling, extremists who stake everything on the desire, fear, love or hate of the moment. I remember tantrums and laughing jags of my own children that more resembled miniature forces of nature than anything human, as impossible to reason with or even understand as a wind or a wave. The adult is mystified and often infuriated by these outbursts, having long ago learned to keep his feelings under control and forgotten what it took to do so. He may feel these small but awesome storms as threats to himself, to the defenses he has carefully built up over the years against the inchoate emotional forces still within him. Also, secretly, he may be jealous of the child's license to let loose. Probably for these reasons, parents and teachers come down hard on children's emotional extremism. They have to repress it in the child in order to repress it in themselves.

These mysterious and messy excesses, however, are part of a small child's testing of his own nature. A tantrum or uncontrolled weeping or unreasonable fright about something or violent expression of anger or hatred are all expressions of deep feelings within him, immoderate and inconvenient as they might be. Feelings of every kind are as much the working capital of a child's personality as is his intellectual and motor-sensory equipment. Punishing him for a tantrum, say, rather than letting it blow itself out or patiently distracting him away from it, is like punishing him for breaking something he is examining. Early childhood is an experimental phase, in which the thing or event itself is everything and the symbol or abstract idea is nothing. A feeling is a feeling, without moral charge, until the child runs up against adult attitudes toward it. The adult who is truly on the child's side will neither prohibit nor punish the expression of strong feeling; neither will he allow the feeling to gain complete control of the child.

As the child grows older, he will begin to learn to curb his emotional excesses, to learn how to channel and control his feelings. It is the parents' and teachers' job to help him do this, a process calling for the balanced exercise of both firmness and acceptance. By acceptance, 1 mean the adult's ability to accept both the child's positive and negative feelings. A child is supersensitive to adults' evaluation of things, and if only "good" feelings are allowable at home or in school, he will quickly learn to mask his "bad" feelings — anger, hate, grief, fear, plus all the confusing combinations, such as feeling love and hate at the same moment. Whatever he is feeling underneath, he will begin to counterfeit the so-called good feelings. In time, he may come to regard negative feelings as alien to himself, as devils within, instead of natural elements of his total personality.

If a child is brought up in an environment that regards self-control as the primary virtue and which looks upon the expression of *any* feeling — love or hate, fear or exuberance — as bad form or even "dirty," he will progressively downgrade his capacity for feeling, coming to regard emotions as things to be on guard against.

All of this results in making a child ashamed of his feelings, or, worse, causing him completely to lose contact with them: many children (and many adults) simply do not know how they feel at any given moment. This numbing of feeling (as Wilhelm Reich and others have pointed out) can lead to a numbing of the body — a stiffening of the muscles and a fear of moving the body that can make even very young children into near zombies.

During one session, I tried a new game with the children, called How Do I Feel? The game was simply having the children decide how they were feeling that day and then doing something to express that to the group.

When treating disturbed children, child psychiatrists often encourage their patients to play out their fantasies and thus reveal their underlying feelings more clearly. Our game, though related to this method, was not designed as therapy but simply as a way to help the children know what they were feeling and in that way to help them know themselves better. We have already seen how Stan and others were able to "perform" feelings that they could never have expressed directly. I thought the new game might encourage more of them to do this. Those ashamed of their feelings might be made less so. They might even end up valuing their feelings more, since the game encouraged them to express them through a creative act which would be recognized and appreciated. Also, they would be using their bodies to express their feelings, learning perhaps to allow their limbs and torsos and all the rest to move with the rhythm of their emotions, rather than remain rigid.

Before we played the game, we talked about feelings. I asked the children if they could name some.

"It's like when you come home and your mother gives you something good you're not expecting, like candy," said one.

"When you take something that doesn't belong to you and your father hits you," said another.

"It's like when you pet a cat."

In my adult-ish way, I had asked the question expecting

70

words as the answers — happy, sad, angry, and so on. What I got back were actual states of their lives — feelings, not labels.

I said that sometimes it is hard to know exactly how you feel. Sometimes you feel a certain way, but you think you *should* be feeling another way. Like when you're really mad at someone — your mother, say — but you smile at her. To play our game, you have to look inside yourself and feel exactly the way you feel.

"Remember when you pretended that you were getting ready for a party? Some of you were sweeping, some picking flowers, some painting the furniture or cooking soup. You had to show us what you were doing and what you were doing it with, and all you had were your hands and your faces and the rest of your body, and your ideas. You really had to *know* that broom or that paint brush or how it felt to pick flowers before you could show it to us.

"Same thing with feeling. In order to show how you feel, you have to first *know* how you feel. You've really got to feel that feeling all the way through yourself. Then you can figure out an idea to show it to us. You can make up a story about it and pantomime that. Or do a dance. Or just walk a certain way. Or anything, just as long as you keep in mind that you're trying to show us how you feel *right now*. OK, now, close your eyes and try to feel how you feel."

As we talked, and before the children had closed their eyes to feel their feelings, Joyce began to retreat — literally. Still sitting on her folding chair, she grasped the back edges of the chair seat, half stood up, and forced herself and the chair a few feet to the rear. She did this again and again until she was halfway to the back wall and still moving. It was like watching a crab scuttling away from danger in slow motion.

Some of the children — I noticed Lucy and Margie in particular — turned their heads to watch Joyce's retreat, but turned quickly back again. They made no comment, didn't change their expression; probably they simply didn't want to have to explain such behavior to themselves.

Joyce was in the rear of the gym by now, her back to us, her forehead leaning against the wall. I felt strongly impelled to call a break and go back and talk to her, but didn't. I felt it was wrong to interrupt the momentum we had, especially at the beginning of a new game.

I gave them a few moments with eyes closed and then asked who could show us how they felt. Stacey volunteered. She lay down on a bench that was on stage. She stretched, rubbed her eyes, sat up, stretched, closed her eyes wearily, and lay down again. Then she more or less repeated the process. At the end of it, she stood up. She paused, smiled at us, and crossed quickly to the other side of the stage; she stood there a moment neutrally. Then she looked up and reacted with pleasure and surprise to something she had received. She cuddled the object, placed it carefully on the floor, and began to stroke it.

"That's easy," said someone when she finished. "You woke up and petted your cat."

"No," said Stacey in her slightly disdainful way, "not quite. I'm feeling very sleepy today because I didn't sleep very well last night. But I'm also very happy because I'm going to get a guinea pig for a pet when my daddy comes home today. I heard them talking about it last night. They're going to surprise me. That's why I couldn't sleep."

Richard came up next. I knew he had been angry about something that morning, so I was interested to see what he would do. He pretended he was playing basketball, shooting for a score again and again, and obviously missing. Each time he missed, he punched the ball with his fist, and each time punched it harder. Finally, after a particularly frustrating miss, he pantomimed kicking the ball away with all his strength, and then stuck out his tongue at it.

Sandy was supposed to be next, but she came over and whispered, "I don't know what to do."

"Well, how do you feel?" I asked.

She looked at me a long time, bewildered and vaguely anxious. She said in a low voice, "Good. I feel good."

I doubt if she knew how she felt. She was trying to find out what I expected of her and her answer was an attempt to appease me, hoping I would not push her somewhere she was frightened to go.

The other children were growing restless. I said to her, "All right. Show us how good you're feeling. Are you feeling very happy or pleasant and nice or just OK or what?" She gave me another long look, in which I read some kind of resentment, and returned to her seat.

Later in the session, she did a skit with several others, in which she played a teacher trying to control her students. The students paid no attention to her unconvincing orders to turn in their homework but ran about in all directions, teasing and making fun of her. Sandy was a passive girl, so she had cast herself according to type. But why had she chosen this particular situation? My guess was that she was getting back at me. She was disappointed that I had not told her how she should feel and what to do, as apparently happened everywhere else in her life. I left her on her own, so she made fun of me with her skit about a silly, indecisive teacher. The giggly, unruly students were what I deserved for not telling her what to feel and do.

When we took our break, I went back to see Joyce. At first, she wouldn't look at me. She kept her forehead pressed against the cool wall on which I was now also leaning. But I could see she was glad I had come.

"What's the matter, Joyce?"

The little half smile that was really no smile at all was on her face as she shook her head.

"Do you feel bad?"

She nodded her head yes, and said, "Yes" in a tiny voice.

"Well, it's all right to feel bad. Everyone does sometimes. Do you want to tell me why you feel so bad?"

She shook her head no, and said, "No."

"All right, why don't you do something for us that shows us you feel bad. You told me once you wanted a cat. Why don't you pretend you have a cat but it's sick and you feel bad about it."

She raised her head and looked at me. "No," she said. "I want to do something nice."

"All right, something nice. What?"

The words came tumbling out. "I want to find a cat from anywhere. I'll pick him up and hug him. Someone comes, a man, and takes him away from me. I cry and I go home to momma. I say, 'Momma, someone took my cat.' She says to me, 'Joyce, honey, I'll get you another cat, don't you worry.' So she gets me a cat and when I wake up, there's my cat. I give it some milk and I pet it. Then I go out on the street and there's the other cat, and now I got two cats!"

Perhaps my sick cat suggestion set off this tale. Or it's possible that it was a favorite fantasy of hers. In any case, it was a complete story, with a beginning, middle and happy ending, with a "snapper": girl meets cat, girl loses cat, girl gets two cats.

74

"That's very good," I said. "Let's practice it."

We did. I played the man who takes the cat away from her; I also played her mother. She quickly became absorbed in the fantasy.

Why had she scuttled away from us like that? I think it was because the game threatened her; she didn't need it, since she already knew too well how she was feeling and wanted to run away from that. What she did need was someone to pay special attention to her. She needed also to forget herself and to be led back to the group. Now, as we rehearsed her tale of the two cats, her eyes sparkled and her body moved with lightness and sureness. She ran fast to pick up her found cat, struggled fiercely to wrest it from the bad man, wept despairingly as she told her momma about her loss, and leaped for joy when her momma came through with a replacement.

She played her skit for the other children without me and did it well. At the end, she became absorbed in the cat her momma gave her and forgot to go back outside and get her first cat back. But it didn't matter. She herself had gotten back.

The next session, Joyce was supposed to help Lucy and Margie do a pantomime, but when their turn came and I looked around for them, Lucy and Margie were whispering together and Joyce was crying.

I went over and put my arm around Joyce and asked her what the trouble was. She just shook her head and buried it in her arms.

I asked Lucy, "Why is Joyce crying?"

She shrugged and looked away. "I don't know."

Margie also shrugged. "She's always crying," she said. When Lucy walked away, Margie leaned over and whispered to me, "Her daddy died."

"What? When?" I asked.

She shrugged. "I don't know. A long time ago." And she skipped away.

After the session, I talked with Lucy's mother, whom I knew was a good friend of Joyce's mother and who brought both girls to the workshop.

"Yes," she said. "Her father died about eight months ago. That poor little girl. She hardly has time to be a little girl. Her mother works and Joyce has to take care of her baby brother. She's almost like a grown woman, that girl. She has her own key and takes care of the house. She has to change her brother and feed him and all — and makes dinner for all of them most of the time too. She's a good cook — better than I am, and I'm not bad." She shook her head. "But it's way too much for a little girl. She's barely eight. I feel very sorry for her."

I suggested earlier that Joyce's skit of the sad bride had some of the quality of a dream. Adults in their world of everyday, hard-and-fast reality dream only when asleep. But a child lives closer to his dreams. There is a reality to magic and miracle and fantasy for the child; he does not so distinctly separate dreaming from waking. He may not know the meaning of his dream, since it is impelled by a secret drama going on within. But he often acts out dreams when awake, and so it was with the sad bride. Joyce's father had fled; he had "stood her up" before she could even wish him hers. So the wedding was a poor one; it celebrated grief. The flowers were tossed away so forlornly because they were not a bouquet of hope, but of loss; more fit for a funeral than a wedding. So at least ran my thoughts upon learning the facts about Joyce's life.

The tale of the two cats also had more meaning for me. They were perhaps "double indemnity" for what had been taken from her. Her fantasy said that something she loved was taken from her by violence. As in real life, her mother was required to make up for her loss. Her wish then was to have the first cat, the original loss, magically restored to her. The fact that when she played it she forgot to go back outside and recover the cat that was taken from her may have been an unconscious realization that her loss could never really be restored.

I knew now as well why I had felt a special sympathy and kinship toward Joyce. I had lost my mother at about the same age that Joyce had lost her father, and my memories connected with some of her behavior. Something pulled at me when I saw the way she gazed up at the stage while other children performed. But I felt it strongest when Joyce began moving backward with her chair in that crablike way. The retreat struck something familiar in me.

When almost everyone else has both parents, and you do not, life seems lopsided. You don't seem to fit in with other children because you don't somehow square with yourself. There is a vaccuum in you that you believe will never be filled. You feel always behind, below or above everyone else, rarely with them or one of them. And never is your resentment of your "queerness" overcome, nor your desire ever satisfied for special attention and sympathy. If only someone understood how you felt without your having to tell them. And you couldn't tell them anyway.

So you always feel like dropping out, retreating, anything but sticking around while everyone is jeering at you. Actually, few do jeer, but you sense a special attitude on the part of your peers. I thought I could see it in the way Margie and Lucy treated Joyce — a little at arm's length. Joyce's set-apartness in behavior fed that special attitude, maybe even created it. In any case, she could never feel she was another child's equal playmate.

The death of her father not only deprived her of the most important man in her life, but also a good deal of her childhood itself. Responsibilities too soon thrust upon this child were barring her from many of the proper benefits of childhood: time to freely play and fantasize, time to "goof off" with friends, and most important, freedom of mind. Joyce was being pulled in two directions: her burden of responsibility drew her toward premature adulthood, while her childhood was fighting for its life. She could be happy for a while playing with other children or pretending by herself, when she could forget everything in the playing and pretending. But sooner or later, she felt compelled to stop herself short. She had to retreat, not knowing quite what she was, afraid of being too much a child when she herself took care of another child.

I think the coat incident was a problem not of straining to conform but of confusion of identity. She was already worried about not being a child among children. Not to have on what others had on would confirm to her that she was a misfit, a queer hybrid, in limbo between childhood and adulthood.

On Valentine's Day, as on Halloween, we took our theme from the holiday itself. I asked the children what Valentine's Day was about. Someone blurted out, "Giving valentines." Margie stood up, rolled her eyes, swung her hips, and said, "It's about goo-goo." The other girls giggled and the boys snickered.

"And what's another word for goo-goo?" I asked, playing the straight man. "What do you think, Donald?"

Donald gave me his usual scared, wide-open-eyed stare but finally said, very quietly, "Love."

"Love it is. So let's do something today about love. What do you know about love?"

"I loved my Raggedy Ann doll when I was a baby," said Lucy.

"Do you still love her?"

She smiled. "I used to sleep with her every night."

"Why?"

She looked puzzled "So I could hug her."

"What else?"

"I kissed her good night."

"And did you say, 'I love you, Raggedy Ann'?"

"Her name was Lucy."

"Oh."

Behind Lucy's back, Richard was leaning over on Stan, pretending to be a doll while Stan was making eyes at him and stroking his hair. Lucy saw them. She blushed and put her hand over her mouth.

"Don't worry about those boys. Would you like to come up and show us how you treated Raggedy Lucy?"

No, she wouldn't like to. The boys had scotched that. And anyway it was probably too much of an invasion of privacy.

"Well, maybe you can do something else later. There are a lot of things to love. You can love a friend, a pet, a place, a toy, something you love to do — almost anything. How do you feel inside when you love?"

"You feel nice," said Betty.

"You want to be with your dog when you love it," said Sandy.

"Just as Lucy wanted to be with her doll. Love is one of the nicest things you can feel, maybe the nicest. A person who loves is very lucky; so is the person who is loved. Why don't you all think of something or someone you love, and then show us."

As with the feeling game, some of the children would not or could not participate freely. Love was too private, too embarrassing; and they were ambivalent about too many things. But others were willing.

Stan repeated his frog-jumping. Frogs indeed seemed to be his first love, maybe his only true and clear one. Sandy stroked an imaginary dog in a stiff but loving way. Then it was Joyce's turn. She came up without hesitation; she knew exactly what she loved.

First, she pretended to watch something huge going round and round. Then she stepped up on something and began jumping up again and again. She stepped off whatever she was jumping on and began running about the stage, first here, then there, finally seeming to bump into something. She repeated this, running about, turning sharply and then bump! Her whole body quivered each time she bumped and then she would shake with silent laughter. She ended that, stepped off, and pantomimed buying a bag of something. She opened the bag and began popping things into her mouth, one at a time. She walked slowly across the stage in a zigzag pattern, chewing and rubbernecking, looking all about with wide eyes as if a hundred enticing things were there.

The other children got it right away.

"She was buying popcorn," one said.

"She was going on the 'lectric bumping car at Coney Island," said another.

"What was this?" I asked, simulating her jumping up again and again.

"I know," said Margie. "That was her on the ferris wheel!"

Joyce's face was glowing, from the happy fantasy she had just been living in and from the interest the children had shown. The workshop "worked" for Joyce. It let her give her fantasies free rein; it made them come true, if only in the sense of playing them out. It gave her the satisfying acceptance of other children, which she craved. It also gave her the satisfaction of creating something for others out of that which was deep within herself. It was an escape for her, an escape for a little while back into her childhood.

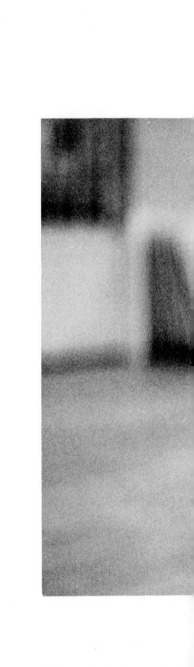

9/ "i am yOur masTer"

Donald — the eight-year-old who had broken down and wept when I made him the pitcher in our abortive baseball game — was sitting on the steps leading up to the stage. His ten-year-old sister Stacey sat just below him, talking to a friend, her long honey-colored hair hanging just in front of her brother. Staring straight ahead and absorbed in what his sister was saying, Donald was unconsciously rubbing a few strands of Stacey's hair between his fingers. It was an affecting sight, the sister functioning as a kind of living security blanket for her painfully shy little brother.

Remarkably, Stacey did not abuse Donald's dependence on her. She watched over him in the group without tyrannizing him or using him to build up her own ego. Donald was too passive to make friends on his own in the group, while Stacey had no such problem. Donald was left on his own when Stacey paid attention to someone else. But I never felt she did so to show her power over him or even because she was impatient with his leaning on her, but only because she wanted to. And she was always there when Donald needed her, and almost always nice to him.

The trouble was, of course, that their relationship was such an unequal one. It's conceivable that Stacey was so sweet to her brother because he gave her so little competition. For the sake of Donald's development, it may have been better if she had been meaner to him. That way, he might have felt compelled to rebel, and rely on himself more. Stacey made it too pleasant to be dependent.

Stacey had worn a long black sequined old-lady's dress to our Halloween session. When her turn came, she did a funny turn as a cackling old crone. She might have been the witch for whom Margie had made the weird soup.

Donald had come in a yellowish lion's mane. I asked Stacey how this had come about and she said that it had been Donald's idea to be a lion and their mother had made the mane out of an old mop. Donald was a fairly handsome boy but he rarely smiled and that day he seemed particularly serious. He had the look of a solemn doe under the mop mane. After Stacey, I called on Donald to play his costume. But he shook his head, as Brent, the would-be astronaut, had done before him. I didn't insist this time. It was suggestive enough that this shy boy should show up in the guise of the king of beasts.

Several sessions later, when we were using the stage for a Guess My Favorite Animal game, Donald couldn't decide what animal to do. I suggested he try a lion, without his mop mane. Again he shook his head. Stacey whispered to me out of his hearing that they had both pretended to be dogs in a game at home that week, and maybe her brother would like to do that. I asked Donald and he nodded.

When his turn came, he got down on all fours, ran a bit, sniffed the floor, ran a little more, and stopped. He looked at me.

"That was good, Donald," I said. "But maybe you should do a little more. Have you ever seen a dog get scared or excited about something and start to bark?" He nodded. "Well, why don't you run and sniff as you did before, but then you come on something that scares you and you bark or yelp. Let's say that table leg over there is what makes you bark. Pretend it's a skunk or a cat or anything you want. OK?"

Solemnly, Donald ran and sniffed once more, until he was close to the table leg. He crouched in front of it and sniffed it, but then he backed off and looked at it. He glanced furtively over at me. I said nothing.

In an earlier session, he had relaxed enough to pick flowers with Brent. And he had performed with his sister a few times, playing spear-carrier roles in her pantomimes. This dog was the first role he had played alone and I was hoping he would be able to do more with it than a quick run and sniff. On the other hand, I remembered the baseball incident and wanted to keep from putting too much pressure on him.

The children seemed restless; Donald frustrated them with his paralyzed hanging back. He was confronting the table leg a little as if it were a snake and he, a transfixed bird. I was about to end the impasse when, surprisingly, his sister called out, "Oh, come on, Don, bark!"

"Maybe just a little bark," I said, unable to restrain myself.

Donald blinked, stared, made a tiny choking noise that

may or may not have been an attempt at a bark — and started to cry.

Too late, I told myself that merely being in front of the group by himself had been a step ahead for Donald. Affected by his tears, I regretted that I had not been content with his running and sniffing. Yet I couldn't help thinking at the same time that Donald would never make real progress without some kind of push. The question was, which kind would help him most?

Quickly, to turn the spotlight away from Donald, I asked the group, "What else do dogs do besides sniffing and barking and running?"

"Scratch," said Sandy.

"Fight," said Stan.

"Sit up and beg?"

"Good," I said. "Why don't we all play dogs." They were up and ready. "Wait," I said. "Donald is going to come down and lead the dog pack in running and sniffing. Watch him and then everyone follow him. After that, see how many different doggy things you can think of to do. Remember what a dog actually looks like when he does those things. Don't be yourself; be a dog. I'll be a person who likes dogs and walk around and call out all the different things you're doing that remind me of a dog."

Tears forgotten, Donald led them in running and sniffing. After that, they lapped water, rolled over, scratched, begged. Two got into a growling match, stalking each other round and round. Another lay on a haunch and an elbow, eyes rolled up, tongue lolling out, panting very doggishly from heat or fatigue.

"Dog fight . . . hot-weather dog . . . scratching fleas . . . wagging tail . . ." I narrated as I walked among the pack. I was glad I had thought to make Donald the sniffing leader. He had enjoyed the other children following him. When I looked around for him, he was softly barking at his sister.

One day during the week after the dog session, Stan and my son Richard had a fight. Both came with me to the workshop session that following Saturday, but they weren't speaking to each other. We had arrived early that morning and the children played with the equipment in the gym to occupy the time before the session began. Richard played basketball with Donald, while Stan, Stacey and others played tag.

Richard had not paid much attention to the younger boy before and playing with him now was only making the best of Stan's absence. However, he seemed to have a good time with Donald, in spite of the fact that Donald was not nearly as good at the sport as he. Or maybe because of it. Richard is quite competitive and enjoys showing his stuff to a boy not as good as himself. Donald tried hard and threw to Richard often. He was happy to gain the attention and acceptance of an older boy whom he admired. The boys talked together as well as played.

After their game, as the workshop session began, a somewhat different air came from Donald. He seemed a little more independent and moved more freely. He was more like someone who knew he took up definite space rather than someone trying to be invisible. He sat next to Richard during the session, instead of his sister.

That day, we again played our version of Simon Says, this time with the children taking turns being Simon. When it was Richard's turn, he came up and boosted himself onto a table that was in front of the group. Swinging his legs, he rattled off some Simon Says orders which the group performed.

I called on Donald to be Simon next, not knowing

whether or not he would come up. He hesitated, staring at me somewhat as he had stared at that table leg onstage. But he came. He climbed on the table, as Richard had done; he had more difficulty getting on top, but made it after several tries. He even swung his legs slightly, as he put the group through their paces. His voice was faint but it could be heard if you strained a little: "Simon says, 'Walk like a duck.' Simon says, 'Be a big bird . . .' "

For the next session, I tried a new game. It was akin to Simon Says but different in tone. It was called I Am Your Master. Each child in turn was to go onstage in front of the seated group. He would say, "I am your master!" whereupon the other children were to stand up. The master would then issue a command, which had to be obeyed. After the order was executed, the children could advance on the master and express their feelings toward him or his command or both. This reaction could take the form of gestures, noises, words or whatever. The only restriction was that no one could actually touch the master.

Stan was first onstage. "I am your master," he said, without much conviction. All rose.

"Be frogs," he said, surprising no one. The children hopped and croaked. Then they approached him, some still hopping, some cheering, some merely shouting for the sheer fun of it.

Richard followed. "Crawl on your stomach like a snake," he ordered. The group obeyed. Then, as one person, they rushed up to him, shouting vehemently and making rejecting gestures. They hadn't liked the humiliation or maybe they didn't like snakes. Half in fun, half in fright, Richard hid from their fury behind the cyclorama.

Ted, a rangy ten-year-old black boy who had recently joined us, was very forceful:

"I am your master!" he trumpeted. When the group had risen, he said, "Be strong!"

Not content with giving the order, he demonstrated how to execute it. He pretended to lift a heavy weight with great effort, slowly and steadily forcing it upward, finally straightening his arms and holding the weight aloft. All followed suit.

He wasn't finished. Now he said, "Be weak." This time he lifted the weight feebly; he couldn't make it; it pulled him to the ground and he collapsed.

Sally, the oldest girl in the group, was next. She told them, "Suck your thumb." They loved that one. When they came toward their master, most of them were still sucking, and cooing to boot.

Margie followed Sally's lead. She commanded, "Be a baby!" They wailed, sucked baby bottles, had tantrums, all with great enthusiasm. When they advanced on Margie to express their reactions, some of them wanted to stroke her.

Joyce's turn: "I am your master," she said in a small unmasterful voice. When they had stood up, she said quietly, "Do what you want to do."

For a few moments, everyone was bewildered; it was a surprising liberation. But they recovered quickly and had a good time doing what they wanted. One wanted to get a Coke from the vending machine in the hall. This was forbidden during the session, so I had to postpone following the master's wish in that one case. When they came toward Joyce, all of them were cheering her.

Peter, who was visiting us, was next. He was a tall, pale eleven-year-old who wore thick glasses. Peter said, "Put your hands over your eyes and walk toward me." They did. But when they got near him, some of them began to jeer. He was a loner, a little erratic in his behavior, who knew no one but me in the workshop. The jeers were probably hostile in-group reactions to a "strange" interloper.

Then it was Donald's turn. I had launched the master game partly with Donald in mind. However, even though he had been willing to play Simon in Simon Says, I did not know whether or not the idea of asserting himself as master of the group would scare him off. After all, he had broken down and cried when he was made the pitcher in our ball game. He had been unable to shout when we had done the shouting exercise a few sessions back.

This particular session had not begun well for him. His sister had found a friend in a new girl named Martha. They had gone off into a corner to plan a skit together. Donald looked stricken and more than usually withdrawn. I took up the slack by getting him into an all-boy pantomime of playing catch that Richard, Stan (they had reconciled), and Ted were rehearsing. Even though Donald was the youngest and smallest, and threw a little "funny," the boys accepted him as a kind of mascot. Donald looked happy playing with them.

So now it was his turn to be the master and it was his choice whether or not to take his turn. He took it. Without any hesitation, eyes straight ahead, his expression serious, he marched up to the stage.

"I am your master!" he said firmly, and louder than I had ever heard him speak. The group rose and awaited the master's order. "Be a lion," he said.

The children roared and sprang, clawed and snarled. Afterward, they came up to him with mixed reactions; some continued to make lionlike noises and gestures, some cheered him, some, exhausted by the game, sat down and rested. I stood where I was and simply admired him. And Donald was smiling a small but definite smile when he came down from his place of power.

Children play out many of their wishes and needs in their games. In the child's everyday world, adults own all the power, and have supreme power over him. Not only do they tell him when to get up, what to eat, what to learn, they also make all the rules and decisions. Rarely if ever does the child decide anything for himself, cause anything to happen, see any impact that he makes on the world.

In the world that *he* controls, however, the world of play, things are more as he wishes them, and needs them, to be. Each child gets a chance to be "It" in a chase game or "Up" in a ball game, and thereby each in turn becomes the first cause, the power at the center of things. In games like Cops and Robbers or Cowboys and Indians, roles are exchanged so that each boy gets a chance to be the "good guy," the hero, the winner.

The child who is master in our game has absolute power, and he can see its effect. He can turn everyone in an instant into snakes or babies or blind people. His image of himself is changed too: he experiences himself as the decider, the commander, the cause of change. He is a slave master, like Simon Legree, but also a magic master, like Prospero, who can raise an Ariel or punish a Caliban.

But the master's power is not experienced in a vacuum. After the master's command has been obeyed, the mastered then have the right of expressing their feelings about it. They can approve, protest, or simply be indifferent. This does not mean the master will enjoy his power less, only that he is made aware of its effect on others. Actually the child can probably surmise beforehand whether his command will be popular or unpopular with the group. Certainly, after he has played master once or twice, he will know pretty well how they will react. His choices of what kind of command to give, and what kind of reaction he wants to evoke, are therefore very wide.

There was another important element of the game, which underlay the rest. The game itself, and each child's power in it, was sanctioned by an adult authority figure, myself. I had delegated my power to each of the children in turn; each was the "master" in my place and with my blessing. The good reaction of the children to this delegation of authority made me realize that this game, as with games children themselves make up, expressed a wish and a need. The need is an important educational one.

To educate a child is in part to give him insight into and firsthand experience with the skills he will need to function in the adult world. For example, a child one day will have to balance accounts, figure budgets, and so on. Therefore you teach him the theories of numbers and give him arithmetic problems to practice on. A child one day also will have to make decisions and wield power, if only over his own life. Power is a much more subtle and complex affair than arithmetic. For that very reason, he needs as much training and experience in the subject as he can get. He needs to know what having power feels like; he needs to learn how to wield it and to take responsibility for the consequences of wielding it.

Since adults hold all power, there is no other way for a child to experience these things except for adults to share some of their power with him. But though many adults recognize the need to do so, the sharing of power runs head on into our own insecurities. We must "protect our authority" at all costs. The idea of giving up a little power evokes the anxiety of losing all.

Yet, if we look at the experience of many adults who deal some power to children, we find that the children respect them more, not less. Far from trying to sweep away the authority of such adults, these children feel closer to them and are easier to guide and work with. We also often find that adults who insist on clinging to all power lose touch with the children in their charge and breed in them discontent, noncooperation and rebellion.

It's not so difficult to see why this is so. The desire for some power over your own life, and for making some impact on the world, is a natural human hunger. It does not appear suddenly in an adult, but is present even in the infant. Refusing to give children a taste of power increases their hunger for it. If a child is denied experience with real power, in later years he might fear it and regard it as something to shun; or he will brood over it, covet it, overvalue it, and regard it as a prize to be seized. In the former case, the resulting passivity can be self-destructive, since exercise of power is a natural function in every human life, and the person who feels helpless inside himself almost certainly is going to become a victim of some kind. In the latter case, when power is seized as an unlawful prize rather than taken as one's natural right in the normal course of maturing, abuse is often the result. One can hardly expect a thief to be responsible in using what he has stolen.

Giving a child practice in power may therefore be one of the most important educational processes. This can take many forms: letting a child make simple decisions for himself, without swaying him with ready-made adult reasoning; letting *him* teach *you* something; putting him in charge of something pleasant — a game or an outing, say — in which he has both power and responsibility; letting him try new experiences — and make mistakes — without moral punishment in case of failure; providing him with the opportunity to create things on his own — from writing a story to building a model to helping to make up a show — creations which will give him some feeling of mastery and in which he can see and feel the impact of his personality on the world.

Above all, the adult must grant power freely and honestly. If it is given grudgingly, the child will feel guilty exercising it. If it is granted with condescension, the child is reduced to a pet receiving crumbs from the table. Better in these cases to keep hold of all power oneself.

Obviously, the needs of different children in this area vary. A girl like Stacey feels comfortable in the world and takes as her right whatever power comes her way. Donald's is a different case. Making any decision or taking any initiative is cause for anxiety in him. He experiences his life as a series of pressures. To keep these from overwhelming him, he keeps himself low, does what he's told, and avoids any confrontations. To Donald, asserting himself in any way is both dangerous and sinful. He could not bear being a baseball pitcher because it made him an initiator of events. He could not shout because shouting is aggressive. The lion was somewhere inside him; the mop mane said that clearly. But it must not be unleashed, even as the bark of a dog.

Forcing Donald to express this hidden self only drives him further underground. The first task, I believe, is to lower his guilt level, so to speak. He needs an atmosphere in which barking, shouting or being a powerful master is the *right* thing to do. He has to be given permission to act out his fantasies, even the fantasy of omnipotence, without having to worry that he will be punished for it.

But permission is not enough. In our shouting exercise, everyone was shouting, which should have been sufficient. Yet Donald could not shout. Nor bark, though he had a lot of encouragement. His guilt and anxiety made it impos-

sible for him to respond, even in atmosphere that said,
"It's *all right* to let yourself go."

Stronger medicine is needed to help Donald. Nothing
less than putting a magic wand in his hand will do, the
wand of Prospero. When he stands before his peers in a
circle of power marked out by an adult — an adult who
represents all adults, who hold all power; when his path
is beaten to that circle by older boys whom he admires and
can identify with; when he stands thus and utters words
that are like a spell: "I am your master" — that magic
wand is his. When the group transforms itself because of
his words, he himself is transformed. He goes all the way
from powerlessness to omnipotence, a giddy experience
that may work on him as a kind of benevolent shock therapy, to burst open some seed of strength within him.

After Donald had turned everyone into lions (and other
creatures too, since we played the game several times in
the course of the workshop), he himself seemed to get
bolder. His very motivation to conform helped him. Under
the shyness was the same yearning for attention and recognition, the love of pretending, the need to communicate
ideas and dreams to others that is in every child. With
everyone else doing funny and interesting things in front
of the group, he felt he could do them too, and "get away
with it."

He continued to play in pantomimes with his sister, but
his roles got better. One skit was his own idea. In this,
Stacey played a parent — or perhaps only an older sister.
She was onstage only a few moments when she stretched,
yawned, and lay down on a bench to go to sleep. Donald
came on, face expressionless, eyes straight ahead, walking
slowly. He climbed on a table and stood on tiptoe to take

something down from a high place. He got off the table, looked around, and pantomimed pouring something into a glass. He drank it and choked a little. (It was a very small choke; you had to watch closely to see it at all.) He climbed back on the table and put the bottle back. Then he jumped down and exited.

Margie guessed, "He was drinking something. He took it down from someplace high up."

I said, "It must be something very special to be up so high."

After a long silence, Donald said quietly, "I was sneaking something."

"What were you sneaking?"

Donald didn't answer, merely looked at me with that mesmerized stare of his.

"It was liquor," said his sister.

The children giggled and Donald smiled without confirming or denying. Was it a special desire of his, to take a swig of his parents' liquor? I doubted it. The liquor probably symbolized a whole range of adult privileges forbidden to him. He wanted to express his desire to break a rule and try one of these privileges. Maybe sneaking the liquor was a cover for something he really wanted to do, but didn't dare express — even within the privileged sanctuary of a skit.

We all talked a little about why we couldn't immediately guess that Donald was sneaking something. We talked about what more he could have done to get this across. I asked everyone, including Donald, to pretend they were sneaking, and they all tiptoed and peered about furtively. I was very pleased that Donald had thought up such a — for him — subversive idea and carried it through.

Several sessions later, we did some work on reactions. After talking about what that meant, each child was to express with his body and face how he reacted when something surprising happened. This time, Donald worked entirely on his own. He sat at a table, chin in hand, studying something in front of him. With his thumb and forefinger, he pretended to slide a small object a short distance along the table, then another, then another, in rapid succession. He was obviously playing checkers, even though he was forgetting to wait for his opponent to move. He took his hand away and studied the board a moment. His hand moved to the table, then he withdrew it, as if hesitating about his next move. Finally, he made a series of jumps, one directly after the other. Again he took his hand away and looked across the table. His eyes were wide and smiling as he jumped back abruptly in his chair. He had won — and he had reacted!

This time the group guessed his pantomime in detail. Returning to his seat, Donald looked pleased with himself. He had a right to be pleased. The magic cloak of pretending, which protects as it exposes, had been upon him. With its help, he had been able to react to his impulse of imagined joy with a real change of facial expression and a decisive movement of his body. It was not a small thing for such a boy.

In fact, this was a hint of something new in Donald. The sneaking skit, and now the checker game, had shown that he had begun to lose his fear of exposure and self-assertion. Out of what he himself imagined, felt, and remembered, he had chosen an idea to play out alone before the group. He had taken command of the stage to communicate very personal elements of himself to the others. It seemed that Donald no longer needed to be handed a magic wand to be a "master."

After a session toward the end of the workshop term, while I was gathering up some material preparatory to leaving, several of the children were putting money in the soft drink vending machine. As I approached the door, I saw Donald standing determinedly in my way. Behind him, I caught sight of his sister Stacey leaning against the wall. She looked offended and forlorn.

"What is it, Donald?"

"Stacey put her quarter in the machine and nothing came out," he said. "She wants a Coke."

I saw to it that his sister got her Coke. It was a double surprise for me: first, that Stacey had chosen to pout rather than handle her own problem. Second, that Donald should take on the role of the protective brother. Perhaps their relationship was not so unequal after all. Or perhaps it was changing.

10/pEOplE picTuRES

The children had been especially enthusiastic about I Am
Your Master. I tried it myself ("I am your master! Be a
motorcycle!"). It was thrilling to see everyone change before your eyes just because of some words you say. It was
magical and satisfying.

But the satisfaction was momentary. I wanted now to
build a broader activity on the theme of transformation. I
was searching for a way to help the children develop more
confidence in their own power to create, a power they
could feel permanently in themselves, not something they
were given for a moment. The things we had done encouraged them to dig out ideas from their private experiences and imaginings and bring them alive with their
bodies, gestures and improvised words. Now I wanted to
give them a way to objectively step back from an achieve-

ment and say, "Look — I did that!" I also wanted them to get firsthand the immediate reaction of the group to their work.

Their satisfaction in this would be something like what they might get from a picture they had drawn or from hearing a poem of theirs read aloud. But ours was the dramatic medium. What it came down to, I realized, was having the children perform the function of a director, who is the shaping artist of the theater. At first such a notion seemed impractical. How could a child be a director?

One afternoon I was looking at a painting by a Connecticut artist and friend named Howard Fussiner. The canvas — in teal blues, vivid yellow-greens and warm oranges and reds — was of a group of figures informally posed around one of their number carrying a ball. I felt some irony in the fact that the sports heroes were featureless: their heads were only colored ovals. But irony was not the artist's purpose. The faces had the effect of minimizing the figures as individuals. They were members of a team but they were also elements contributing to a unified composition.

Yet feeling was in the painting as well as form. Vigor and camaraderie came through in it, a kind of essence of team spirit. Infused in the painting was the artist's memory of his boyhood admiration for strong, skilled players united as brothers to capture glory.

What struck me was how Howard had transformed a visual cliché — the ritual team snapshot — into a refreshing piece of art. He had been able to do so, I believe, because he retains some of his original vision of the world — "original" both in the sense of first or earliest, and in the sense that it is his own.

These reflections led me toward a new project for the workshop. A child sees the world with his own eyes. What he sees is different from what anyone else sees. But few children value their own special way of experiencing things. It's easy to scare or ridicule them out of it. They are persuaded to take on someone else's vision with little difficulty.

Yet it is just his own eccentric vision which makes an individual grow into himself. It is also the source of original contributions to society. The objective should be to help a child value it, not give it up. If you give a child a medium that is easy for him to use, to play with, he might show you something of what he sees. If serious attention is paid to what he shows, he himself will value it more. Perhaps eventually he will go off on creative flights that will surprise even himself.

But first he must find that comfortable and reassuring medium. Kenneth Koch in his book *Wishes, Lies and Dreams* talks about the difficulty he had in loosening up his primary grade students so they could write poetry of their own. First, he had to break down the "Keep Off" fences that made poetry the property of a special few. For example, he told the children that they need not use rhyme or meter. Then, to start them off on poems of their own, he had his class write a group poem, in which every line should begin with the words, "I wish" and should contain a color, a comic-strip character and a city or country. The resulting poem excited the children. It was evidence of their own power to create and it opened up for them a completely new way of expressing what was happening in their lives. Koch proved again that children "drop out" of a subject because they give up on it. It's "too hard." It's "no fun." The answer is not to make it easy but to make it interesting, to make it accessible to their abilities, and to connect it with their lives and feelings.

Other gifted teachers I had heard of — such as Emily

Dennis at the Metropolitan Museum in New York and Susan Sollins in Washington — had helped free children to create in the graphic arts. These teachers brought children closer to art by encouraging them to *impersonate* a work rather than merely look at it and talk about it. I wondered if I could turn this around somewhat and use some of the conventions of art to help the children in the workshop create in the dramatic medium: they would make pictures on the stage, using the other children as their "materials." It seemed something they could easily do, since they would begin with just what they saw in the world and they would work with other children whom they knew. And I knew it would be fun for them to actually see their ideas come alive before them.

I called the game People Pictures and we played it at the next session. First, we discussed what kind of pictures they liked to draw. Their favorite subjects were animals, houses and people, in that order. We talked about sculpture, too. All of them had worked in clay or plastic or had made shapes in mud and sand, so they quickly understood the idea of three-dimensional art. We also talked about how an artist or sculptor can use any subject he wants — something he's seen or dreamed or just thinks up. When he begins to work on his picture or sculpture, it will change as he goes along, since his idea about the subject changes. But he will work on the idea until it's as close as he can make it to what he finally decides he wants it to be.

"In our game," I explained, "each of you will take a turn making a three-dimensional picture. The group here will be your paints or clay. The stage is your frame — what the picture goes inside. The artist will take as many people as he needs onstage with him to make his picture.

"The subject of your picture can be anything you want.

Maybe it's a picture of people skipping rope. Or people at a funeral. It can be a dream you've had or a wish you've always wanted to come true. It can have animals in it or a robot or a magic tree. It can be funny or sad or even crazy, if you want. No one in your picture can move or talk, so the picture has to tell us everything.

"When the people you need to make your picture are on the stage, close the curtain and tell each of them what you want them to be. Tell them exactly how you want them to stand or lie or kneel down, where their hands and feet should be, what the expression on their faces should be. If any of them are not just right, change them. The people in the picture will have to remember that it's the artist's picture. He's thought it up; he wants to be proud of it. So everyone in the picture should help him by doing just what the artist tells him to do. Remember, everyone gets a chance to be the artist.

"The artist probably shouldn't be in the picture himself. He'll want to be able to see it out front, and anyway, he'll have enough to do making the picture.

"Pictures have titles, or names. Does anyone know the name of a famous picture?" I got back Whistler's Mother and the Mona Lisa. "Good," I said. "Thinking up a title may help you organize your picture, give you a clearer idea of what you want your picture to be. It will also help you make it just one subject.

"When your picture is ready, stick your head through the curtain and call us. Those who aren't in the picture will be playing a game, so you'll have to call us loud. Then open the curtain, come down, and we'll all look at your picture. We'll applaud if we like it. Don't tell us what your picture is, let us guess. After we guess, maybe we'll talk about it a little. If we have any ideas about improving it, we'll say them. That'll help the next person have a better picture, maybe."

I paused. For all my explaining, some of the children still looked puzzled. I happened to glance at Stacey and saw that she understood perfectly. In fact, she was all ready.

"Stacey, you look like you've got an idea that can't wait. Why don't you do it, to get us started."

She picked out several people, including her brother Donald, took them onstage, and closed the curtains. I was fairly confident they would do all right without adult supervision. I now had an assistant, and could have sent her with them, but I decided to see what would happen. My assistant, Randy Goldfield, a graduate in educational drama from NYU, led the children who were not in the picture in a game while Stacey was creating behind the curtains.

Stacey alerted us she was ready, the curtains opened, and here is what we saw: Lucy was sitting on a high stool, her back to us, her legs gracefully crossed, her chin raised slightly. Behind her and facing us in a rough semicircle were several other children: one was peering intently at Lucy, looking undecided. Another, one eye closed and right arm outstretched, was measuring Lucy with her thumb. Another held an imaginary writing or drawing instrument in her hand and was poised to use it. Still another was holding something away from herself, the better to appraise her work. The children auditing the picture guessed the subject quickly: artists drawing a model. Stacey pointed out that she had made a picture of people making a picture, and we were off to a clever start.

In fact, I regretted having spent so much time talking about the game. Stacey's picture of the picture-makers had been worth a lot of my words. Now everyone understood what to do, and in almost no time, everyone had a picture in mind. They drew numbers for turns. I asked them to let Randy know how many persons they needed to make their picture, so she could assign them. It was Randy's thought to do it this way rather than let the children choose, feeling that the same children might be chosen over and over, and some would be left out. She told them not to worry about whether the people were boys or girls, unless there were a special reason to use one of the other. This was said because there were more girls than boys in the group. She told them girls could take boys' parts where necessary, and the children didn't protest this.

Ted's picture was next: stools and chairs were overturned across the stage. Stan and Richard were angrily squared off at each other near the center. A prone body (Betty's) lay close by the battlers. Martha was standing facing them a few paces away, her palms clasped together in supplication. Donald, frozen in a running position at the left, had two fingers of his left hand near his lips, blowing something. The index finger of his right hand pointed accusingly at the brawlers. And Amy was high up on a ladder, at the right, her hands pushing against the back wall of the stage. It was a well-composed and balanced picture which told a dramatic story.

The other children guessed it was a fight; someone was hurt or dead and someone was begging the fighters to stop. They also guessed, after a few moments of trying, that Donald (of all people) was a policeman about to arrest the fight and the fighters. The artist-director did have to supply the answer to one question: what was Amy doing on that ladder?

"Holdin' up the walls," said Ted. "Those guys are really breaking things up."

Ted also had to supply the exact locale, which he did with his picture title: "Breaking Up the Diner."

Ted lived in a small suburban town, sharing three rooms on top of the local post office with four brothers, two sisters and his parents. He was a rough, energetic and alert boy who had spent the first eight years of his life (he was ten) in Bedford-Stuyvesant.

When he was the master in our previous game, his first command had been: "Be strong!" His second was, "Be weak!" Now, in his picture, he did not show us the fighters and the policeman alone, although they would have made a complete tableau. The violence had a context: The inert body was the consequence of the fight. The supplicating figure struck a note of conscience, compassion, reason. And the holder-up of the wall introduced a relieving note of ironic humor.

Clearly Ted was more than the rough, merely alert boy who met the eye. He had sensitivity too, and an awareness of life as having several levels of behavior and feeling. As in a dream, where the dreamer is himself everything he dreams, so the characters and actions in Ted's "people picture" were all parts of himself. To create his picture, he first had to sort out some of the conflicting emotions he felt in himself — cruelty and compassion, for instance. He also had to objectify different modes of behavior he had observed in life. The compositional balance he achieved in his picture was matched by a psychic balancing, an ability to order and reconcile conflicting feelings and varieties of behavior. He was able to fit the parts into an integrated whole, and in doing so, he must have felt a surge of inner satisfaction and power as a creator.

With Joyce (the sad bride), the scene became more peaceful. Her picture was a fashion show, with models posing, a photographer crouching, and a few bored ladies viewing. When we talked about Joyce's picture, Stacey commented that the artist was using only half the stage. It was true. The models were all bunched at the right, close to the fashion-show viewers. The rest of the stage was bare. Sally said that all the models were doing the same thing. She was right too.

I asked Joyce to take another look at her picture and see if she wanted to change it. She shook her head. I asked if she minded if Sally and Stacey did something more with it, and she shook her head, which I took to mean no, she didn't mind. Stacey placed the models so that they were evenly spaced in an informal semicircle across the stage. Sally varied their poses. She put one model's hand on her hip and tilted her chin. She had another place one leg well in front of the other and lean back. And so on.

I asked Joyce if her picture pleased her more now and she said, "It's not my picture."

And so it wasn't. Joyce's direct reaction made me realize that it had been a mistake to interfere with her picture. If that was the way she saw life that day — lopsided and monotonous — then that was just the picture she should have created. Talking about her picture was one thing, but to have allowed other children to "edit" it so as to conform to a more "balanced" or "interesting" picture was just the way to undermine Joyce's confidence and pride in her own special way of looking at things.

Richard's picture was next. When the curtain opened, a child was sitting cross-legged on the floor, shoulders shrugging, arms out, palms up, in the classic pantomime of "Who cares?" Another, however, did care. He was standing nearby raising a clenched fist, his face glowering with anger. Another looked as if she were making a reproachful speech to another child, who was hanging her head. Two others were sitting on a bench, one with his head in his arms, the other merely looking dejected. And one, who gave it all away, was taking a vicious swing at an imaginary ball with an imaginary bat, reliving a past moment so as to change a high fly into a home run.

Sandy, in the audience, said: "It looks like they lost the game."

Richard nodded. He said his title was, "We Lost."

I had not mentioned to Richard that Howard Fussiner's painting of a team had set off the idea for our new game, so at first I thought it a little uncanny that he should have picked such a similar subject. But remembering Richard's preoccupation with sports, I felt his theme was not necessarily chosen because of any telepathic connection with me. The specific subject of his picture did interest me though. Richard hates to lose, whether at cards or baseball. Why then didn't he pick "We Won!" rather than "We Lost!"? Perhaps his picture was a form of preventive magic. The baseball season was close at hand. If he conjured up in his picture the worst that could happen, maybe it would appease the devious gods of sport, deceive them into believing he didn't really want to win. Or perhaps he simply picked the more dramatic subject, feeling that a losing team would make a better picture than a victorious one. To paraphrase Tolstoi: "All winning teams resemble one another; every losing team loses after its own fashion." In any case, he had successfully projected a number of the modes of losing.

Sally's picture had a certain epic sweep. At stage left, a seal (Robin) was caught in an eternal moment of flapping its flappers. Next to the seal, an elephant (Ted) was squirting the keeper (Stan), who was in the act of throwing the seal a fish. In the center, a woman (Martha) was buying a balloon for her child (Margie on her knees) from a jolly balloon man (Donald), whose balloons were lifting him to his tiptoes. At the right, a gorilla (Richard) hung dolefully from a bar of his cage. And far upstage, high on a ladder, a noble lion (Betty) presided over it all. Sally had made good use of her entire "canvas" to set a panoramic summer scene at the zoo.

Donald must have admired Sally's lion, although he didn't comment on it. He himself was content with a more intimate subject, a *tableau vivant* of the game of Keep Away, or Monkey in the Middle, as it's sometimes called. He had forgotten or disregarded the rule that the artist should not appear in his own picture and had cast himself as the person in the middle. Two children were frozen in the act of keeping the ball away from him, while he was reaching up to intercept it.

It was hard not to interpret Donald's picture as the projection of one of his leading inner images, especially as he had insisted on putting himself in the middle of it. He felt himself as indeed the "Monkey" in the middle, small and easily victimized, while things were being kept away from him. (I was put in mind here of his "sneaking" pantomime as well.) On the other hand, he was not passively giving up, but striving to pull down the prize. And maybe he would.

11/ TURN ABOUT IS FAIR PLAY

The workshop now made up a coherent "people picture" of its own. No longer a random collection of children, it functioned in many ways as an organic group, with a life and a spirit of its own. Brent and Carrie had dropped out, to my disappointment. But a solid core of regulars remained, in which the newcomers — Ted and Martha — soon found a place. In the beginning, the children had been reticent to do anything with anyone not a friend or sibling. But now, though friend still preferred the security of being with friend, any child in the group could work smoothly with any other. They still poked fun at each other's mistakes, but all jeering had stopped. The more self-confident children now occasionally included the more standoffish ones in their games and pantomimes. Actually, whereas in the beginning the group was threatening to some of these more reserved children, now they derived support from it, especially when they performed. There were arguments, even fights at times, but that only showed that the relationships developing were total ones. They even had inside group jokes.

One Saturday, we played a game I had wanted to try for some time. It was a game that required mutual trust and, among other benefits, had the potential to deepen that trust. I borrowed the idea from the adult Theater of Encounter in New York City, which I had attended one summer evening. As its name suggests, it is half theater, half encounter group. A troupe (or group) of performers leads the way in acting out their feelings and problems; then the playing area is thrown open for anyone in the audience who wants to do the same.

The evening at the theater had opened with everyone pairing off to play a game. One member of each pair shut his eyes and the other led him around. The theater was a huge loft, with a central arena surrounded by platforms piled on top of other platforms. There were many places to crawl under and climb over, many textures and props to explore. The "sighted" member of each pair was encouraged to expose his "blind" charge to as many different experiences as he could devise, including exploring other people they met along the way. After a while, the roles were exchanged. The leader became the led, and vice versa.

I had enjoyed the experience and felt that it would be a good thing to try with children. I experimented with my own children and they were delighted with it. I thought the children in the workshop would enjoy doing it too, since it would be a "scary" new game. It would also give them the experience of exploring familiar things as if they were brand-new. It would help them develop trust in themselves and in one another. And it would be an interesting experiment in role-switching, in which each child would alternate being the leader and the led.

First, we wanted to get them into a relaxed and trusting mood. Randy led them in a game she called Rag Doll. She showed them how to shake themselves out and get "all loose," starting with head, neck and shoulders and ending with knees and even toes. After a while, most of them really did have the look of loose-limbed Raggedy Ann's and Andy's.

One of them said, "I feel like when I get up in the morning."

"I feel like I want to go to bed," said another.

"All right, do it," I said. "Pretend the floor is your bed." Some very carefully laid themselves down on the floor. Others went directly down, as if really falling into bed.

"Now that you're in bed, turn over on your backs. But don't go to sleep. Just relax," I said. "Now, I want each of you to give me your head."

That got giggles. I had done this exercise myself in a class at the New School conducted by Charlotte Selver. I had learned that it isn't easy for an adult to "give his head" to someone. However, I thought the children would have little trouble with it.

"Why do ya' want my head?" asked Margie, the jokester.

"I just want it."

"Maybe you won't give it back."

"I'll give it back."

"You might bump it."

"I promise I won't. Randy and I will go around and pick up each one of your heads and hold it for just a minute. Then we'll put it back down, very gently. Don't help us, and don't *not* help us — just give us your head. Now close your eyes and we'll be around."

It was a nice feeling, to heft the small heads, each unique in size, shape, weight and texture of hair and skin. The energy of the young spirits flowed into my hands. Most of them gave their heads with confidence and ease, including Margie. She had had no real qualms. Her head felt light in weight and moved pliably from the neck when I lifted it.

When I picked up Joyce's head, I knew she was actually feeling the distrust that Margie had jokingly expressed. She was afraid and tried to control her head. I could feel tension and resistance in her neck.

"I'll take good care of your head, Joyce," I said softly in her ear. "Don't worry about it — just let me borrow it for a moment."

She let go a little, but never really confided her head to my care.

Donald was even more stiff-necked and wary at first than Joyce, and I talked to him as I had to her. Suddenly, his neck went completely limp, so that his head was a dead weight in my hands.

I said, "It's a head, not a rock. It's a good head too, with good things about it. Good eyes and ears outside and lots of interesting thoughts inside. Remember all those good things and then give them to me. I'll take care of your head and give it back." The small blond head relaxed and got a bit more headlike.

Now I thought we were ready to move into the "blind" game. The children had trusted themselves enough to let their bodies go loose and relaxed. Most of them had trusted us with their heads. Now perhaps they were ready to trust one another.

I had been a little reluctant to try this game before, because I didn't know whether the younger and less disci-plined children could be completely trusted to guide another child in such a situation. For instance, I worried that Margie might carelessly do something in fun that would endanger another child in her charge. My ultimate feeling, however, was that given responsibility for another person, they would all acquit themselves well.

We divided the group in half and Randy paired them off. She showed excellent judgment in doing so, pairing children who had not had much direct contact with each other, but who would be likely to get along in the game together. Wherever possible, she put a younger child with an older one. I had decided to use blindfolds, to avoid the temptation to peek and also to make it more like games they knew, such as Blindman's Buff and Pin the Tail. To demonstrate the game, I put on a blindfold and Randy led me around a few minutes. She had me touch a window ledge, go up the steps leading to the stage, and sit down.

After I removed the blindfold, I told them, "Remember, when you are the one who's leading, your partner can't see. He's got to trust you to take care of him. Only you can tell him there's one more step to take or there's a wall right in front of him or whatever.

"The fun is to show your partner how everything feels without being able to see it. Give your partner as many different things to do and feel as you can think up — as long as he's safe. In a little while, we'll switch around."

Few things we had done at the workshop worked more smoothly or gave more satisfaction to the children. Or to me. It was good to see the pride of the leaders, especially the younger ones, as they showed their partners around, eyes bright with attention. The blindfolded ones were wary and tentative at first, but quickly began to enjoy being led. Several of the leaders were quite resourceful in thinking up interesting things for their partners to do. One pair ran together. A leader had her partner throw basketballs into the air. One of the bigger children got down on all fours and directed her smaller charge on how to mount and ride her. Two couples met and the "blind" members of the pairs felt each other's head. The most popular feat of all was climbing the short flight of stairs leading to the stage, no doubt because it was the "scariest." There was a soft mat on the stage which several children felt and lay down on.

Afterward, I asked the children which they had liked best, leading or being led; and what they had liked and disliked most about the experience. Here are some of their reactions, which I taped:

Ted: "I like being the leader, 'cause you could get 'em all scared and make 'em feel nervous . . . think they're going to bump into somethin'. I liked walking on the mat and feeling it. It felt funny." *"How do you mean, funny?"* "You know, soft." *"You like soft things?"* "Yeah."

Joyce: "I liked being blindfolded best. It felt fun; I like tripping and stuff. I didn't like being a leader, 'cause I don't want to lead people. The bad thing I liked is walkin'. I don't like to walk." *"Why not?"* "I don't know."

Sally: "I liked leading. . . . I told her there was no more steps but she kept putting her foot up high 'cause she was sure there was another step. It was funny. I was afraid when I was being led. It scared me most when we started running."

Donald: "I liked being blindfolded. I liked going on the stage. I liked the soft part." *"Were you scared to be led by someone when you couldn't see?"* "No, I wasn't scared." *"Did you trust your partner?"* "Yes."

Stacey: "I liked best being led, because it was sort of mysterious. You kept wondering where she was going to take you next. I liked leading, too; it was fun showing her

around. We both took each other up the stairs. There were
a lot of stairs — we kept telling each other to go up, or
stop, stop!"

Martha and Margie were paired, and Martha had
shared my apprehension about her mischievous partner. I
asked her: "Did you trust your partner?"

"Ye-es," she said, and then, "No, not really."

Yet when I asked her which she had liked best, being
blindfolded or not, she replied, "Blindfolded. I kept tripping on the stairs, but that was fun. . . . It didn't seem
like you were in the same place at all."

Margie had managed to find a little trouble for her partner. She had taken Martha into a small room that ad-
joined the gym. The room contained a pool table.

"I didn't like that table," Martha said. "There were bits
in it that come out and prick you. I kept touching them."

Margie said, "I liked best being blindfolded, 'cause it
made me hurt my toes when I couldn't see nothin'. It was
scary. It seemed to be getting darker all the time." "*Do you
like hurting your toes and being scared?*" "No . . . yes."

Lucy's younger sister Tanya, a tiny six-year-old, was
visiting us that day and had played in the game. Randy
had paired her with an older girl, a tall visitor named
Jackie. It was Tanya who, as a leader, thought of letting
her "blind" giant partner play with some basketballs that
were lying around.

Tanya said: "I liked not being blindfolded best. I liked
leading her because when she was leading me I felt like I
was still a baby."

Jean Piaget says (in an interview in May 1970 *Psychology Today*): "The egocentric child — and all children are
egocentric — considers his own point of view as the only
possible one. He is incapable of putting himself in some-

one else's place, because he is unaware that the other person has a point of view."

In our game, the child switched points of view when he switched roles. As the blindfolded partner, he was helpless, dependent, childlike. When he was the leader, he was powerful, responsible, parent- or teacher-like. As the leader, he had the ideal means to put himself in someone else's place — that is, the adult's place. He was charged with complete responsibility for another person for a few minutes, to be his eyes, his watchdog, his guardian. No amount of lecturing about "responsibility" would have brought home the meaning of that idea nearly as well as those few minutes. And we have seen that some of the children actually preferred that role. To quote Piaget again: "The child must discover for himself through his own activity." By actually *being* the responsible party, the child discovers for himself how it feels to be responsible; he also may learn that responsibility has its own satisfactions.

In later sessions, the children did improvisations which involved more sophisticated and sustained role-playing and role-switching. I supplied general premises to get them started. One of these premises was as follows: Character A has something that Character B wants. Character B has to try to persuade Character A to give it to him or share it with him. But Character A should keep what he has until he feels persuaded to give it up. Or, it could be something Character B wants to *do* but Character A does not. Then the roles would be switched and the story begun again. I gave them some examples but asked them to make up their own situation and roles, pick someone to play with, and improvise dialogue and movement. I told them I would interrupt if I thought it was necessary.

Stacey did such an improvisation with Robin. Robin was the eight-year-old who had played the hysterically laughing child to Stan's fall-down clown. She and Stacey played two children at a park lagoon, meeting for the first time. Stacey was sailing her two boats on the lagoon; Robin had no boats and wanted one.

Robin: "Can I please play with one of your boats?"

Stacey: "No, they're mine." Stacey's tone was not arrogant, but indifferent.

Robin looked at me and shrugged. "She won't let me play."

I asked her, "Robin, have you ever gotten candy or money or something you wanted from someone who didn't really want to give it to you?" She nodded. "Well, that's what you have to do here. We know that you want a boat. You've *established* that. (We had talked about "establishing" things.) Now what you have to do is to persuade Stacey — prove to her that you really like boats and try to convince her that she should let you play with one. And remember, both of you, that you're telling us a story, a story about two girls and two boats. Each of you is telling half the story by how you act toward the other."

Robin started over. She said, "You've got two boats there. Do you need both of them?"

"Yes, I do," said Stacey, pretending complete preoccupation with her sailing.

Robin looked at me again, but I didn't say anything. I could see that this wasn't easy for her. She didn't like the tension of waiting and persuading. She wanted to get it over with. But she was a game girl and now picked up the challenge of the story herself:

Robin: "I've always liked yellow boats."

Stacey: "So have I."

Robin: "I like red boats too."

133

Stacey: "Well, I don't care."

Robin: "I'll hold your boats when they get to the other side. I'll take them out of the water for you."

Stacey: "I can do that myself."

Robin: "Well, do you mind if I just watch your boats? I like to just watch you playing with them."

It was a subtle stroking of Stacey's ego as well as a play for sympathy. It was not cleverness, though, but Robin's natural way of approaching such a situation. In any case, Stacey had to respond.

Stacey: "No, I don't mind, if you want to."

Robin: "My mother almost bought me a little boat like that one but she didn't."

Stacey: "Well, I have lots of boats at home."

Robin: "Are they all red or all yellow?"

Stacey: "All different colors."

Robin: "Well, if you have so many, maybe I could play with one."

Stacey: "Well, when they get over to the other side, I'll let you play with the red one. I like the yellow one best anyway."

Then they switched roles, with Robin owning the boats. But turning the tables didn't change Stacey's confidence that things naturally came her way. She opened up the new dialogue not with a request but a statement:

"I'd like to play with one of your boats."

To which Robin responded with a rush of words: "Oh, yes, why don't you come home with me and I'll give you any boat you pick out. I've got lots!"

Again, Robin had not been able to bear the tension, this time of holding out on someone.

I said, "You're a generous girl, Robin, and I can understand how you want to share your boats. But remember you're helping to tell a story. A story means that something has to happen, something has to change. Our fun is to see that change happening, to watch you take us from what is to what will be. You own the boats now and Stacey wants one, as badly as you did before. You should make her work a little to persuade you this time, so the story can be told. She won't really mind waiting. Do you want to try it once more?"

Stacey: "I'd like one of your boats to play with, please."

Robin: "Which one do you like?"

Stacey: "I like the yellow one."

Robin: "All right, I'll go get it for you and we'll play together."

I didn't pursue it further. That was the way Robin felt. Moreover, she apparently identified too strongly with the "have-nots" to dare put herself for long in the place of a "have." But, at least in the first improvisation, she had succeeded in overcoming her tension enough to help tell a story. She had played herself with resourcefulness and grace.

Stan and Richard did one, each trying to persuade the other to do something he wanted. Richard is playing ball by himself. He's bored. Stan enters.

Richard: "Come on and play baseball with me."

Stan: "Can't. Want to go catch frogs."

Richard: "How about hockey?"

Stan: "Naw. I might get hurt."

Richard: "Marbles?"

Stan: "Rather play with frogs."

Richard: "Why?"

Stan: "Oh you can watch 'em hop and catch 'em and give 'em to people, and hear 'em go 'Yeuch!' "

Richard: "That sounds good. Let's go catch some frogs."

Then they switched roles.

Stan (plugging the imaginary ball into his make-believe mitt with real conviction): "Wanna play baseball, Richard?"

Richard: "Nah. I might get hit in the head."

Stan: "How about football?"

Richard: "Might get hit in the stomach."

Stan: "Hockey?"

Richard: "Might get hurt in the foot. Rather play with frogs."

Stan: "What's so great about frogs?"

Richard: "Well, they're squishy and slimy and feel good. They sorta feel like you."

Stan: "Oh, yeah. Well, I don't wanna play ball with you anyway. I'm gonna go catch some frogs."

It had a nice Tom Sawyer-ish quality. The boys had borrowed ideas from each other but put them to work each in his own special way. And they connected one idea to the next, a good exercise in logical progression.

Lucy and Margie played out a universal mother-child confrontation: a mother wants her daughter to get out of bed and go to school; the daughter resists. Lucy played the mother first, using gentle persuasion to get her daughter up. Margie, thumb in her mouth (not merely a piece of "stage business" on her part), was a stubborn and bratty daughter. She finally got out of bed but then ran around and around, dodging and hiding to avoid going to school. Eventually, however, she settled down, ate her breakfast, and went.

Then the roles switched. Lucy, as the sleepy daughter put up her resistance mostly in the form of taking her time getting dressed, plus some muttered back talk. And what a no-nonsense disciplinarian of a mother Margie was! She shook her daughter and yelled at her to "get out of that bed right now!" She threatened her with drastic punishment if she didn't hurry up. She told her she'd get her father after her.

Margie's explosive "daughter" turned into a most explosive "mother"; Lucy's quiet, gentle "mother" became a quiet, gentle "daughter." It's not surprising that young children, still very tentative about who they are, should play themselves in such an improvisation, whatever the role. But within their personality range, they can identify very closely with someone else. Lucy's "mother" was gentle, but as she went along in the role, an air of firm authority began to come from her — so strongly, in fact, that her bratty "daughter" bent to her will and went to school. Margie also turned into an authority figure, albeit a tyrannical one.

Piaget may be right in the absolute sense when he says that "the child considers his own point of view as the only possible one." But it is also true that children are always "trying on" other points of view through role-playing. When they "dress up" or play a pretend game, the outer changes — costume, facial expression, voice, gait, etc. — reflect a powerful inner picture. Moreover, they believe in their make-believe roles. Both Joyce and Margie were quite convincing in their roles because they were serious about them. Neither would have dreamed of making fun of her own part or her partner's or the situation. That would have stopped the fun of the pretending, which demands conviction. And within the game, each moved beyond her usual point of view and took on a new one.

Taking on a new point of view is not always possible for a child, however. We saw with Robin that she could improvise a scene as a girl without boats but not one with boats. The latter role threatened her. When their own unresolved problems are involved, young children rarely have strong enough egos to play out such a scene. It is better they do not, since illusion and reality are too easily confused in their minds and serious disturbance may result.

Older children, however, often have the willingness and the egos to play scenes with close-to-the-bone content, but they sometimes get "stuck" in the problem. I saw a number of examples when I conducted an improvisational class some years ago with a twelve-to-fourteen-year-old group. In one, two twelve-year-old girls improvised a scene in which one was a mother who wants her daughter to take piano lessons and the other was the daughter who balks at the plan. The "mother" used all variety of rather silly but plausible-sounding adult reasons: They had just bought a new piano and it had to be used. They knew an inexpensive piano teacher. The father had played the piano. Playing the piano is good for a girl. Her tone was adamant and authoritarian. The "daughter" on her side refuted one by one all of her mother's points, all to the effect that she would not even consider taking piano lessons. *Her* tone was adamant and nasty-rebellious. When it got to the "You will!" — "I won't" stage, I interrupted them.

"Mother," I said. "You were once a daughter, right? Can you think of any reasons why your daughter might *like* to take piano instead of why she *must* take it?"

They took that in and tried again, but absolutely no sweet reasonableness flowed in. After another brief discussion, I had them switch roles. Again, the same showdown psychology took hold of them both.

It would have been easier to understand if one or the other, or both, had been improvising their home situations. But I happened to know both mothers, and I doubt if this was the case. Confronted with such serious opposition from their daughters, either mother might easily have drawn back. But even assuming there was a conflict at home, why was it that when each of the girls had a chance to play the mother, neither one softened her stand against her "daughter-self," as I had suggested? Why didn't they "show up" the bad parent by playing a better one?

I came to the conclusion that the piano confrontation was altogether too close to their own problems in growing up for them to play it as anything but melodrama. An imaginative leap is necessary to put yourself in another's place. These almost-teen-age girls were too involved in their need to separate themselves from their parents to make such a leap.

To them, the lines were drawn. Regardless of their own personal experience, they insisted that a mother stand on one side of the "generation gap," a daughter on the other, and each yell across her hostility. To become her own person, a girl must wrench from her parents the prerogative to order her own life.

Something like this, I believe, was the way the girls felt. If the "mother" in the improvisation had been sympathetic, it would have spoiled the justification to tell her off. So each girl unconsciously accommodated the other by playing the part of a mother fury. Their instinct was to use the improvisation to express what they were feeling in real life. It was a chance to rebel with maximum force and minimum risk. They were not playing in a story; they were acting out a fantasy of defiance. Maybe it served them as an escape valve in the overheated generational conflict.

Whether or not role-switching is involved, improvisations provide children with several good learning opportunities. Safe within the sanctuary of pretending, children can take a step toward learning how to express their feelings. Improvisations also help them learn to think on their feet and help teach them how one idea can lead to another.

By taking a principal role in a story, and helping to make it up as they go along, children are actually exploring the *nature* of stories; they learn about conflict and characterization by embodying them. John Dewey strongly believed in dramatic play and improvisations as learning devices. Many social studies teachers today use the improvisational method as a learning aid. One elementary school teacher told me she had cast three of her students as Columbus, Ferdinand and Isabella and let them play out the threesome's crucial meeting on how to finance Columbus's trip to the Indies. The teacher said her class still talks about it; it's one historic confrontation they won't forget. Another teacher I know had two children improvise a scene between a slave-owner and an abolitionist, as part of a unit on the Civil War era. The scene between the two got pretty heated and led to a lively class-wide seminar on slavery, with many usually quiet students participating.

Improvisations also can give children some insight into how relationships actually develop between people. Since an improvisation involves an arbitrary premise and is put on before an audience, it is not "natural." But it also involves two different personalities, each with his own motives, experiences and problems, confronting each other in a relatively freewheeling situation. Each improviser must make continual spontaneous decisions on how to respond to what has been said to him. Each such decision has a consequence, which is the further response of his fellow improviser. In these respects, improvisations are at least roughly analogous to dialogues in "real life" relationships. In both cases, one never really knows how it's all going to turn out.

With children, the trick is to allow freedom of expression and provide impetus when necessary to keep the scene going, while at the same time helping them keep their feelings from getting out of hand. Young children naturally need more such assistance than older ones. They need a strong galvanizing premise related to their own experiences to start them off. To keep them going, it also helps to give them an objective to shoot for: e.g., talking someone into giving you something you want.

But whether tightly structured or not, an improvisation has strong built-in suspense value. An audience doesn't know what's going to happen next in a well-joined scene; so they will no more lose interest in it than they would in a street fight where the issue is in doubt. That is why one can usually count on even young children paying close attention while a protagonist and an antagonist chosen from their peers improvise their story.

12 / A good vehicle

A crusty Santa went about, peering over the shoulders of his toiling helpers — dollmaker (Betty), train-tester (Ted), puzzle-deviser (Amy), and all the others. He grumbled about how hard it was to find good help these days and made each helper show his project to him and describe its construction. The more toys Santa saw, the less cranky he became. Finally, he called jollily for his sleigh, and half of his eager helpers transformed themselves into eager reindeer. They flew out into the snowy night to visit children in many lands. These children, also former Santa's helpers, woke one by one just after Santa dropped in. They opened gifts Santa had left and expressed their feelings about them.

It was our first group improvisation, which we did just before Christmas. The holidays are an especially vivid and dramatic season for children. The world is transformed into a place a little more to their measure and liking. The dressing up and colorful religious pageantry, the touching story of the infant Jesus, the Santa myth of generosity, and the fact that adults are more indulgent toward them, even play with them more — all are part of this transformation. Children sense that the holidays are their time of year and feel a little special to themselves during them.

So our improvisation had a particular zest and flow. The children were completely caught up in it and everyone participated (including myself, playing Santa). We moved all over the stage and gym. Santa's helpers, reindeer and Christmas-morning children played scenes in many different corners. The helpers had to decide which toys to make, and later, whether they wanted to turn into reindeer or gift-receivers. There was freedom in their movements, yet they paid attention to details as well: most of the reindeer pranced rather than galloped across the clouds, a doll was created small and fragile when it came out of the wrapping, and the girl who created it (Lucy) reacted with nice surprise and wide-eyed pleasure.

All of them got involved in the story. Their animated faces reflected that special satisfaction children get playing smoothly together in a group. And each made a contribution. The format itself encouraged more individual creative spontaneity than the group games we had played previously, with their rules about who does what and when. "Creative spontaneity" can get a little out of hand at times, however, when children get overinvolved and forget the difference between pretending and "real life."

For instance, after the success of the rope-skipping session, I had been encouraged to try a related improvisational activity. The rhythm of the rope had set going a group rhythm. Each child, whether turning the make-believe rope or jumping in, felt that rhythm and manifested it. Each new jumper extended it. Each player seemed to feel pleasure in giving himself over to the beat of the imagined rope and the entire group seemed bound together by it. I wanted to try translating this experience into an improvisational rhythm. A protagonist and an antagonist would be chosen, analogous to the rope-turners. They would set the beat by disputing some issue or other. Then other children would "jump in" one by one, on one or the other side of the argument. Theoretically, the alternating disputants and their seesaw arguments would set up a rhythm of their own, which all would feel and respond to. Note I said "theoretically."

The premise we used was this: a girl is picking flowers on a field which is private property. The property owner catches her. When the improvised scene began, the issue of private property versus personal liberty was debated with some religious overtones:

"They're my flowers, y' know."

"They are not!"

"Okay, whose are they then?"

"They're God's!"

"Well, they're on my property!"

"Who says it's your property — God?"

The trespasser who had God on her side now got a little moral help from a friend who jumped in. Together they lectured the property owner on his selfishness. The owner countered by calling in a policeman:

"Hey, dontcha know it's against the law to cop flowers that don't belong to you? I'll have to take you to jail."

"You leave my friend alone or I'll tell my father."

"Go ahead and tell him. He's nobody."

"He is too. He — he's the mayor!"

"He is not!"

"He is so!"

"Well, ok, my father is the President."

"He can't be. You're a grown-up and if he was the President, he'd be too old. He'd probably even be dead."

"Well, you have to come to jail anyway."

But now someone else jumped in.

"You can't take my daughter to jail."

"She's stealin' flowers from this lady, so she has to go."

"You leave her alone. She's beautiful and she never stole anything in her whole life."

"Oh, yeah. She stole my flowers. There. See? Look at them, right in her hand."

"Well, who says they're your flowers — God?"

By the time a teacher and a hippie had jumped in on the flower-picker's side and a principal and a rich woman on the owner's side, the scene began to disintegrate. I had asked that each pair of disputants talk to each other for a few moments and then, when a new pair jumped in, move to one side and continue their argument in pantomime. But as the children got more deeply involved in the situation, they forgot, and continued to make points to each other without regard to new arrivals. As the pitch of the argument rose, they stopped listening to one another altogether, and soon everyone was talking at once. No group rhythm had appeared; in fact, I heard only a noisy dissonance. With the improvisation approaching the outskirts of Donnybrook, I called the whole thing off.

The Santa improvisation had worked more smoothly because, for one thing, there was more physical than verbal activity. There was also a more familiar story core that defined appropriate action and speech for the children. Finally, where the jumping in activated the group's antagonisms and spirit of competition — and aroused its pride too — the Santa scene tapped its participating and cooperating spirit, allowing each child to contribute his individual "bit" and then smoothly reenter the group.

Still, despite its failure to provide me with a rhythm, and even with its touch of chaos, I still believe the "jumping in" kind of idea has possibilities. For one thing, I like its very ability to arouse and vent the children's partisanship, as well as its potential to help reason out beliefs. I think the idea would be more workable with a smaller group. With only one or two jumping in on each side, they could develop their reasoning at length, rather than be continually distracted and interrupted by other debaters eager to enter the fray.

Randy Goldfield, my assistant in the workshop, contributed an idea that led to a very satisfying group improvisation. As with most good ideas, it was simple and basic and suggested others of its kind. Like the Santa improvisation, it centered around an activity that the children already knew about and which loosely structured both group and individual action. In addition, it had promising improvisational possibilities and offered a wide range of role-playing choices to the children.

The idea was a make-believe bus trip in which a bus driver makes several stops to pick up a variety of passengers. By the way the passenger goes to the bus stop, boards, relates to the bus driver, pays his fare, and finds his way to his seat, he makes a great deal known about himself, including age, occupation, mood, and special idiosyncrasies. After he has settled down into his seat, he pantomimes his character until everyone on the route has been picked up. Then he may contribute to whatever events take place on the loaded bus.

Before the bus ride, Randy and I led them in some

games and exercises that would help them establish the roles they chose to do. Early in the workshop, the children tended to imitate the broad stylized movements of TV and movie actors or the caricatured actions of cartoon characters. Their early story ideas often derived from TV and movies as well. I encouraged them to make their own observations of how living people, rather than pictures on a screen, move and react. We worked on creating roles through the use of small gestures and movements, rather than broad, gross ones. The use of the hands, arms, legs and face was demonstrated in reproducing the little details that, taken together, can shape the image of a personality.

Now we built on this by having the children establish different characters by their different ways of walking. How does an elderly person walk? A teen-ager? A lame person? A fat person? A fat person with a heavy burden? Each child tried each type of walk, and did others that he thought up.

Since many of them would want to carry things on the bus in order to establish their part, we did some further work on pantomiming objects. Each child had to establish the weight, size and shape of an imaginary stone by the way he picked it up and gave it to someone else. Some selected a pebble, some a flat skimming stone, some a huge boulder.

We asked each one to walk along a make-believe street, find something, and establish what it was and how he felt about it. The other children tried to guess the found object and when they did, the finder gave it to someone else. The latter had to dispose of it in some way and then go find something of his own. These skills, and others, were put to use on the bus ride.

The first role to be cast was the bus driver. At first, I

thought Randy or I would have to do it. The driver would have to keep the improvisation as well as the bus moving along. He would have to react in some way to each person who boarded his bus, to help the character establish himself. He would also have to be the "captain of the ship," keeping some order on the bus, answering questions and settling disputes with some air of authority. I wasn't sure any of the children would want to take all this on.

I was wrong. After Randy had explained the part, Stan quickly volunteered. I would never have guessed that this diffident frog-lover would come forward for such a role — partly because I did not believe he would want to put himself out to this extent, but also because it was an authority role. I had always felt he was a little wary of me because I was too much an authority figure in his eyes. The feeling that he was uncomfortable with authority was reinforced in my mind when I watched him play the role of a school principal in an improvisation. He had been silent and resentful in it, not holding up his end well at all.

When he raised his hand to volunteer for the bus-driver role, I had the private thought that he would not have done so had I still been conducting the workshop alone. Randy, a warm and attractive woman of twenty-one, had brought something out that I had not seen in him before. Partly it was his awareness of her as a pretty woman. But also he seemed more *there* when she was involved, more alive to what was happening when she was leading the group. I think it was Randy in particular who drew him out, but also I guessed that he generally related better to women than to men (though it's hard for me to be objective about it). In any event, it was plain to me that he saw the bus-driver role as a way to show off his male resourcefulness and qualities of leadership and authority to Randy.

148

As it turned out, he handled the role quite ably. He didn't engage in much give-and-take dialogue with the passengers, but neither was he flustered by any of them, even the "kookiest," nor by any of the goings-on that took place in his bus. He handled emergencies and answered questions with dispatch and self-confidence, the very model of the cool, competent, no-nonsense bus driver.

Before Stan took his bus out, Randy and I worked with those who wanted help in choosing or developing their roles. We made only one rule before we began: wait for your turn. Don't talk when someone else is "on."

The first passenger was at the bus stop. He was a professional strong man (Richard), who came on flexing his muscles and showing them off to the bus driver. However, he got tangled up in his dumbbells trying to pay his fare. A fussy mother (Robin) and her two wailing children (Margie — again, she was on her knees — and Betty) were picked up next. While the mother was protesting the high fare, the two little ones crawled all over the bus. A wounded Vietnam veteran limped on, very bitter and raucous. (This was Stuart, a visitor, whose parents, interestingly enough, were both very active in the antiwar movement.) A hippie (Ted) boarded just behind him, smoking something suspicious. Immediately, he and the veteran got into an argument. The hippie accused the vet of tripping him with his crutch.

The fussy mother complained to the driver about the disturbance and demanded her money back. Meanwhile, her children were crawling all over the strong man. The bus driver tried to settle the argument, but it got more and more heated. A policeman (myself) appeared to settle the fight and persuade the combatants to calm down.

A tiny drunken lady came on then (Tanya, visiting us again, and again resourceful). She lurched convincingly down the bus aisle and fell across the seats. She had not paid her fare, which aroused the driver. She was in no condition to talk to him, so he called the policeman. The cop asked her to walk a straight line; she couldn't, so he took her off the bus to sober up.

A foreign lady (Sally) came aboard. Everyone knew she was foreign because no one could understand what she was saying. In fact, the language she used ("Strack Branus clum fargot . . .") was pure improvise-ese. Someone on the bus, however — the fussy mother it was — happened to understand and translated for the benefit of the driver. The foreign lady made a lengthy speech of thanks, or something, and paid her fare in foreign money. Two other ladies, very rich and uppity, came on gossiping (Joyce and Lucy). A boy came on, very straight, with the tiniest of smiles on his face. (This was Donald. When I asked him later who he had been playing, he said, "A happy boy.")

A mysterious, shifty-looking passenger (Stacey) had been picked up earlier in the trip. She kept changing her seat, making implausible excuses each time — it was too cold in one place, too stuffy in another, or the children were too pesty. After a while, she wanted to get off; in fact, she insisted that the driver let her off, right there and then.

After she had gone, the strong man discovered that his dumbbells were gone. The fussy lady couldn't find her purse. The veteran was missing his crutch. The foreign lady shrieked in her untranslatable tongue about losing her jewelry. Everyone accused the person who had just gotten off of being a pickpocket. There was an uproar and I (the policeman) was fetched. I chased the alleged crook up the street, caught her, and retrieved all the booty. While I was giving everything back, the pickpocket slipped away. One by one the passengers left the bus, with a parting comment to the driver. All but the hippie; he had fallen asleep. At the last stop, the bus driver looked around and saw him. He went back and woke him up. The hippie smiled, lit up, and offered the bus driver a drag. The bus driver refused self-righteously and escorted the unsteady boy to the exit.

So it went, with many starts and stops, and some bumpy going along the way. While the improvisation was going along, Randy had kept up a running commentary on the action, utilizing ideas the children came up with to push the story on, trying to keep everyone involved without letting anyone get "stuck" either in argument or silliness. Her narration spotlighted what each child did, giving the work of each some recognition and importance. It also had the effect of tying each part into the ongoing saga. My policeman functioned as a cooling-down element, to be used when the temperature of the action rose too high. Also, I enjoyed getting into the act.

The children exchanged parts the following session and it was a completely new improvisation. The bus had proved a first-class vehicle for us. It also served as a kind of trial run for the simple show we were scheduled to give at the end of the workshop cycle, with the parents of the children, church members and other interested parties in attendance.

13/ TO SEE THE CHILDREN

We gave our show after a church supper. While I was getting my plate filled in the church kitchen, the sparkling-eyed matron who served me asked: "What are the children going to do for us tonight?"

I smiled and said, "You'll see." Then, remembering the kind of semi-improvised show they were about to do, I added, "And so will I!"

"Well, it doesn't really matter, does it?" she said. "We all just like to see the children."

To see the children. That is indeed what we like when they perform. To see them move and speak and pretend. To enjoy their eagerness and their spontaneity. To watch them, even though they are a little scared, a little self-conscious, bask in the lights and the attention. If we're lucky, we might catch a glimpse of the inner life of children, their life of play and their marvelous ability to believe in what they are doing.

But how rarely we actually have this charming experience. In most of the elementary school shows I have seen, or heard others speak of, the children seemed too anxious about remembering their lines and movements to be natural or spontaneous. Their voices sounded mechanical and droning. Even in moments of crisis in the play or pageant, their excitement seemed almost programmed. In musical shows, too, the singing and dancing sometimes seemed to have been rehearsed to such a point that little of the children's natural rhythms were left to enjoy.

As they watch their children perform in such shows, the parents' pride is often marred by anxiety that the child will forget or garble something, embarrassing himself and them. If the child has a lead, his time onstage may seem to last forever to the tense parents. After he is offstage, the parents may breathe easier, perhaps even look about to see if everyone has noted the performance. But when they sit back, they prepare not to enjoy themselves but to be bored.

If ever an activity of children should be unboring, it is a show they do. Many parents remember the awkward but delightful off-the-cuff performances their young children put on for them at home. But there is about as much fun watching children being put through their paces in a show as there is in listening to them recite their multiplication tables.

Perhaps the tension and the boredom, the dearth of joy in the whole proceeding, will be set down as the necessary price to pay for "giving the parents what they expect," and for adequately demonstrating the school's resources and effectiveness. Unquestionably, many schools feel real pressure to stage only the traditional, carefully planned and thoroughly rehearsed type of show for an open house or end-of-term presentation. Anything less would not seem serious. But it might be that parents, if alerted in advance to something new, will find more satisfaction in a show in which they can really "see the children," as the lady in the church kitchen put it. A hint of this is what happens when a child actually does make a mistake in a show: bumps into another player or dancer onstage, gets his tongue twisted over a difficult line, or draws a complete blank, makes a face and stands as if mesmerized until the hoarse whisper from backstage gives him back the forgotten words. Then tender smiles break out, and warm laughter — not because anyone is enjoying the player's discomfiture — but because the inner child has broken through at last!

As for demonstrating the school's resources, a show would more aptly do so if the show in turn demonstrated more of the *children's* resources — their spontaneity and creativity, not just their ability to memorize and be directed. One might protest again: how can you demonstrate spontaneity and creativity if the show is to be professional? The answer is, it shouldn't attempt to be. A professional actor can give the illusion of naturalness even when everything he says and does has been carefully practiced. But rarely a child. Someone said that the faculty of memory is one of the weakest in the human psyche. If so, it must be weakest in the youngest. It stands to reason that the less a child has to worry about forgetting lines, cues and a plot, the freer he will feel and the more spontaneous he can be. And the more a child is involved in creating a show and shaping his role in it, the more motivated he will be to help make it a good show.

The reason some school shows prove enjoyable is just because the director has managed to let the children's *unprofessionalism*, their natural gift for make-believe, come through the script. In these cases, the script is usually minimal and the director has not been afraid to share some of his power with his cast. Sometimes the children are even allowed to write the script, which is rarely professional but almost always charming in performance. But now, on to *our* show.

When I first conducted a workshop of this kind some years ago, I felt that having to give a public performance would not serve my basic purposes. As far as younger children were concerned, the forms of theater were mainly occasions to help children realize themselves in various ways. The stage served as an outer platform to coax the children to play out their inner fantasies and ideas. I knew of course how children love to put on shows, but I felt they would have one another for an audience and that would be enough for them to handle. Performing for an outside audience of adults, including their parents, would create too much anxiety. The tensions of the theater were all right for actors, but I was not training actors. Also, I was concerned that the prospect of a show would throw the workshop out of balance. Rather than keeping foremost the spontaneous flow of work and play, everything we did would be shadowed by the looming "show business" finale.

The children taught me differently. Or rather, I was right about the workshop, but wrong about the show. My first workshop was attended by two hand-holding friends: a nine-year-old Argentinean girl and a ten-year-old Polish girl. Neither of them asked any questions or reacted in any way while we were talking about what we were going to do. I was all through outlining the program, and about to start a game, when I saw the Argentinean girl raise her hand. The Polish girl reached up and brought her friend's hand down, frowning at her the while.

"You have a question?" I said to the girl who had raised her hand.

Both girls shook their heads.

"Both of you don't have a question."

They giggled. Then the Argentinean girl blurted out, "When are we going to give the show for the people?"

I explained that we were going to do a lot of things that would be fun, including acting things out for one another, but giving a show was not that important for us at this point. I did not feel I had completely closed out the possibility, but it was enough for the girls. They never came back.

My initial reaction to this was to regret that the show-business mentality set up by TV and the movies was strong enough to cause these girls to deny themselves a potentially good experience. Nothing was worth their while but the prospect of being "stars" in a production in which they would be watched, admired, perhaps even envied.

I realized later that mine was mainly a defensive reaction. It was natural for these girls to believe that "acting out things" led to "giving the show for the people." In their experience, what other result could there be? But more important, if the desire to be in "show business" really was their motivation, then my job was to move with that. TV and the movies are among the strongest influences in the lives of children. So be it. I thought about how I could ride that interest to benefit the children.

I saw how an audience of children watching one of their number perform gave a performer the valuable gifts of attention and recognition. They helped a Margie channel her show-off energies into creative effort. They helped a Donald and a Lucy come out of themselves. They gave a Joyce some feeling of group acceptance. They gave a Carrie and a Ted good reason to reach into their secret selves and communicate what was important to them. I wondered if giving a show for adults wouldn't give the children things their peers could not supply, that would be worth the tension they would undergo: a recognition by the grown-up world of their achievement and mastery, a chance for their parents to see them in a new light — as independent performers. I also foresaw they would draw together more closely as a group if their small world was about to be exposed to the big one. The church, which sponsored the workshop, had been encouraging me to give a show, to gain more interest in what we were doing. I decided to try one.

We developed the show during the last few sessions of the workshop. First, we talked about what the show should be, discussing and discarding several ideas. One child had done a touching pantomime of an old lady who takes a pill and turns into a young girl. I suggested we expand that idea into a tale whereby several old people are visited by a magic imp, who turns them all young. Betty said we should pretend it's an old folks home, such as her grandma lived in. Sally said her mother had some old-fashioned dresses in their attic and let's do it in costume. Margie said she wanted to be the imp. We were on our way.

We talked about the differences between being old and young. I defined the word "stereotype" for them and said that rather than imitate a *stereotyped* old person, they would give much better performances if they first observed how real old people, such as their own aged relatives or people they saw in the street, acted and sounded. As they had done before performing the bus improvisation, but now concentrating on the specific needs of the show, the children practiced walking, talking, gesturing, even arguing, in the contrasting modes of youth and age.

When I had suggested expanding the original pantomime into a show with many old people, I had been a little concerned about monotony. But as they began to work on their characterizations, I was reassured that there would be as many different old people as there were children.

The improvisational quality of the show that began to develop was true to the spirit of the workshop. Yet the nature of the project demanded some reorientation. Obviously, the workshop atmosphere could not be preserved in the presence of an outside audience: how can you be spontaneous in an improvisation when your parents are watching you? And we had to take into account the point of view of the audience: they have to know what's going on as well as the players. So some kind of structure was needed, in order that everyone onstage would know generally what was going on. And some rehearsal was needed, so that the children could communicate what was going on to the audience. Actually, structure and rehearsal were essential if the children were to feel some sense of freedom on the stage during the show. It would hardly do to replace one tension, that of having to remember a plot and your lines and movements, with another, that of having to make up something under the pressure of an audience's attention.

The idea was to preserve maximum spontaneity and freshness within a minimum structure. We had set the general outlines of the story: there would be several groups of "old folks" in a parlor of an old people's home. Each group would take a turn at entering, gossiping, arguing, and so on, then drop off to sleep. The magic imp would enter and transform the first group into young people. They would waken, react to the change in themselves and one another, "act young" in some way, and exit.

Then the next group and the next. We would figure out an ending later.

This structure seemed to leave plenty of room for improvised characterization, dialogue and action. It also eliminated the need for leads. In such an episodic story, everyone could be in it, and no one child (or small number of children) would have to carry the burden (and/or the glory) of telling the story. By the same token, it would not be disastrous if someone didn't remember what to say or do. Even if a performer were struck dumb, the show could go on. There was a need to remember a few cues, so that the show wouldn't stop dead, but that seemed a minimum amount of memory work.

The children began to form groups and improvise dialogue. It is in the early stages of developing a show — especially the kind of show we were engaged in — that a director most needs his faith in ultimates and must pay the least attention to present chaos. There was a good deal of arguing, balking, pouting and plain wandering about, as the infant show crawled toward its unknown destination. Despite our previous activities, some of the children found improvising difficult. Their everyday experiences just did not give them much confidence that they could make things up, but rather encouraged them to follow instructions. When they asked Randy or me what to say or do next, we would first try to make suggestions that would help them move forward on their own. But a few absolutely required that they be told what to do or say.

In a surprisingly short time, however, the show began to take hold. In the beginning, some of them had felt that the idea we had chosen was "dumb" or "corny." But as the dialogue and action took on firmer shape and they could sense a flow and totality to the story, they became more interested in the show as a potentially successful enterprise, and in their part in it. The balking and arguing and wandering began to recede. In their improvising, they began to tie in with one another's lines and actions. And the need to make up the show was causing them to dig deeper into their creative capacities. Some even contributed ideas beyond their particular roles, ideas which improved the show as a whole.

Stacey, for instance, had noticed that all the old people complained of the same ailment — a backache. She suggested that each person take on a separate infirmity: one would have a limp, another be hard of hearing, another have bad eyes, and so on. This helped vary the characterizations, and also, when the imp had transformed each old person into a young one, he or she could express a different form of relief or liberation from his special complaint.

Another example of a child's contribution moving a show forward: Robin loves rock music, and thought up the idea of having her group of old ladies overhear a Beatle number from across the way. The ladies got up creakingly to hear the music better. Lucy, who was in the the same group, began to move to it.

"Old people don't dance," said Joyce critically. Lucy stopped dancing.

I said, "Maybe not, but I'll bet some old people would like to dance. Let's see how you old ladies try."

They started to dance, slowly and ponderously, as old ladies might. Robin stopped dancing and said, "I used to *love* dancing when I was young. I sure wish I could dance like that again."

Which was a nice setting up of the transformation that was to come and also suggested a line of dialogue development for other groups. They could talk about what they used to be able to do but could no longer, now they were old.

And, as with Stacey's suggestion about varying the infirmities, Robin's idea pointed to specific acts they might perform when they turned young. I brought a record player to the next rehearsal session and, when Robin and Lucy's group ran through their transformation scene, they were able to dance, with youthful joy, to the real sound of the Beatles.

In making her entrance with her group into the old folks parlor, Sally lagged far behind the others. She was so old and bent, in fact, that the others had to take hold of her arms and shoulders and seat her bodily. Sally had long hair and had loosened it so that it almost completely covered her face. She didn't say a word behind her waterfall of hair. All that came from the "old hag" was an occasional cackle. In point of fact, Sally was the oldest in the group; it occurred to me that she was merely preserving her seniority in the old folks home.

The other "old girls" in Sally's group made up for her silence. They were confirmed gossips and went on at a great rate about their daughters, their sons-in-law and the awful new generation. Then they turned to the old men.

"Look at them," Amy's shrewish voice whined. "All they ever do is play cards. Cards, cards, cards. Dirty old men never pay attention to anything but those dirty old cards." (A cackle from Sally.)

Sure enough, on the other side of the stage, the "old men" had no eyes for anything but their card game:

"Two hearts," said Stan.

"Three hearts," said Donald.

"Ten hearts," said Richard.

I asked them what game they were playing and they said they didn't know. They had heard something like this on TV. I said it might be hard to carry this on very far unless they knew how the game was played.

"Can we play Go Fish?" asked Stan.

"Fine." Besides solving their problem, I foresaw that it would be entertaining for an audience of adults to watch children pretending to be old people play a child's game, and it turned out that way.

"Do you have any threes?" Stan asked Donald.

"Eh?" Donald had decided to be a hard-of-hearing old man.

"Do you have any threes?" Stan repeated.

"What?"

"DO YOU HAVE ANY THREES?" Stan shouted, holding up three fingers. "THREES!"

"Oh," said Donald. "Why didn't you say so? No. Go fish."

When the card game got repetitious, I asked if there was something else the old men might talk about. Richard got it started.

"I saw Nixon on TV last night. Boy, he stinks."

"I think he's good," said Stan.

"President McKinley was much better. You'll never die in your bed with Nixon. He's got the air all polluted."

"It's not his fault. I think he's good. I think McKinley stinks."

They were leaving Donald out so I interrupted. "What do you think of Nixon, old man Donald?"

"I like Nixon," said Donald.

Richard said heatedly, "Oh yeah? He stinks!"

Donald looked intimidated and fell silent. His sister Stacey got up and whispered something in his ear. Donald stood up and said to Richard:

"I think that's a terrible thing to say about our President!"

Richard looked at him and then said, "Well, I'm going to take my medicine."

When Richard had gone to the water cooler, Stan said to Donald, "I think that old man cheats."

"I know," said Donald. "Well, all this getting mad makes me tired. I'm going to bed."

During a rehearsal, just before she was due to come out as the magic imp, Margie first stuck only her head out and rolled her eyes. It was very implike. When I praised her for the idea, she sucked her thumb. Again, after she had touched a group of the sleeping old people to change them to youngsters, she sat on the edge of the stage to watch them, instead of exiting as expected. It was just what an imp, hating to miss the fun, would do. The next time she ran through her part, Margie forgot about sticking her head out first, but she had a new "bit." Grinning, rubbing her hands together, and walking pigeon-toed about the stage, she launched into a long monologue about how she was a very naughty imp, how she was going to play a trick on all these old people, and how she was going to laugh at them because they would be so silly when they got to be young. It looked to me as though Margie might function as a kind of impish *raisonneuse* who could tie everything together.

Joyce, however, was a problem. The sad bride was balking at being a member of the show. She was in Lucy's and Robin's group, but said almost nothing. During the rehearsal, she insisted on sitting with her back to the audience. I told her privately afterward that she didn't have to do or say anything if she didn't want to, but if she turned her back to the audience, they would think that was part of the show.

"Well, I'll be an old lady who doesn't want to talk to anybody," she said. I let it go for the moment.

Feeling somewhat apprehensive that we were trying to put on a show with too few rehearsals, I called a double session the Saturday before the show. I asked the children to bring their lunches that day; we would then have plenty of time to run through the show, eat our lunch, and then play a game before we rehearsed again. The children liked the idea of bringing their lunches.

During the first part of the double session, before lunch, Joyce looked particularly troubled. She again turned her back when she was onstage. I said to her, "Joyce, you can't be part of the show and not part of the show at the same time. You have to make up your mind." She turned around obediently, but only went through the motions with the other girls.

We had lunch in the small room off the gym. The children's lunching together was an incidental necessity due to my calling a double session, one in the morning and one after lunch. But there is something intimate about eating together, which children in particular feel. In school usually only best friends will lunch with one another, and lunchtime connotes to children time-out, unfettered conversation, a chance to have fun. This was the first time the children in the workshop had ever eaten together, and from what happened, I realized that the lunch itself brought them closer together as a group.

As a matter of fact, I was sorry we had not done this kind of thing earlier. Even though we played games and had fun together, the children "worked" in the workshop; that is, we had a regular series of scheduled activities. I could see from the simple event of their lunching together how much these children enjoyed and benefited from getting together in a natural social setting. Conversation flowed, exchanges took place, and relationships moved forward in ways not possible in even our lightly structured situation. If we had done it earlier, it would also have helped me. I would have been able to observe the natural role each child took in a group and to decide, based on seeing the group together in a relaxed mood, which activities might work with them and which might not.

They told one another stories and jokes while they ate. Stacey turned out to be a *raconteuse* of mysterious murder stories. Munching their sandwiches, the other children listened raptly to Stacey's tale of an evil Chinese jade figurine with long fingernails who could imitate perfectly the voices of each member of the unsuspecting family that owned him and, by this subterfuge, bloodily wiped them out, one by one. Then she told one about a boy who had drowned at his summer camp, and haunted the camp year after year with his ghostly cries for help. It all sounded morbid to me, but the children relished the tales as much as their dessert cookies.

Eating lunch and talking with the other children was cheering up Joyce, I noticed. She even told a story, one about a black cat who loves tangerines so much she learned to peel them. Someone put poison in one of the tangerines and . . . The children gave her their total attention.

Right after lunch, she and Lucy went out into the gym to play with Stan. He chased the girls all around the gym. Then the three of them played Keep Away. Later, Joyce came running into the room where Randy and I were still eating. Her eyes sparkling, she said, "Do you know what Stan just did?" And she tumbled over her words as she told us all about the fun they were having.

After a while we went back onstage for a rehearsal. During the morning session, Robin had been doing most of the talking in her old ladies group, which included Joyce. When we resumed after lunch, Robin began to take up where she had left off, reminiscing about "When I was little —" But things had changed.

"When *I* was little," interrupted Joyce, "I remember how it was. I liked to do a lot. I liked to skip. I liked to jump. I liked to run. I liked playing with my sailor doll too. It felt good to do that . . ." She went on for some time, staying in the character of a fondly reminiscing old woman, telling about "how it was."

When she ran out of breath, she turned to her friend Lucy and said, "Why don't you say something now, Lucy?"

When we gave the actual show, Joyce said very little. She didn't turn her back, but she had tightened up again or else the audience made her too self-conscious to be able to contribute much. But the day of the double session, she had eaten lunch and told stories with the other children, and a boy had paid attention to her and played games with her. She had been happy and, afterward, she could remember how it was.

The second part of the show, when the old people were transformed, was easy to develop. The children had only to ring changes on themselves. When the imp transformed Lucy, she did an admirable skip all around the stage, exclaiming softly, "I'm young again! I'm young again!"

Martha woke up after the imp had done her stuff and looked at Betty:

"What are you doing here? You're not old."

"Well, you're not either."

"Yes, I am, too."

"You are not."

"Yes, I am!"

"Just go look in the mirror. You're a kid, not an old lady." (Pause, while Martha looked into a make-believe mirror.)

"You're right, I'm a kid. 'Ray, I'm a kid!"

"Me too!"

To give themselves a natural exit, each one was to discover his favorite mode of transportation just below the stage, run down the stage steps to mount it, and then away to the exit at the back of the gym.

"Look, a bike!"

"I see a motorcycle. Watch me ride it!"

"Watch *me* drive that Mustang!"

Sally and Amy, the oldest girls in the group, decided they wanted to revert all the way back to infancy when the imp changed them. They practiced sucking their thumbs and crying. To get themselves offstage, and as an audience-participation fillip, they wanted to wander down into the audience to seek their mommies. After sitting on the laps of a few women who only *looked* like their mommies, they were to find their true ones and sit on their laps. The girls admirably kept this surprise from their mothers until the show itself, so the mothers' reactions to this "bit" were genuinely improvised. They laughed, hugged their daughters, and enjoyed being in the show.

When the old men were transformed, there ensued a comfortable reversion to the boys who had been underneath all the time:

Stan: "Oh, boy, now I can go catch me some frogs. I'll swipe that canoe."

Richard: "Hey, c'mon, Donald. Let's go play catch."

Donald and Richard did a good pitcher-catcher pantomime. Then they discovered a Sting Ray and a pair of skates to take them off and away.

Ted had played a lone hand during rehearsal. As a bent old man, he had gone around feebly snapping his fingers, and once in a while pantomimed gyrating in slow motion with an electric guitar. He was reliving his youthful days as a rock star. When the imp had finished her youth-making work on him, however, he expressed resentment rather than pleasure.

"What a drag!" he exclaimed looking at himself in the mirror. "I don't wanna go through my whole life again. I'll just get deaf and have all those girls kissin' me and huggin' me."

Ted's variation suggested an appropriate ending for the show, which we had been looking for.

"Well, Ted," I said. "You'd better find that imp and get her to change you back."

"Where's that imp?" He found her backstage and dragged her with him. He demanded that she change him back.

"I don't know how," said the imp.

"*You* know how."

"I know, but I forget."

"If you don't change me back to an old geezer again, I'll throw you in the Hudson River. And that's *polluted*."

"Oh, yeah?"

"Yeah!"

I intervened. "I know a magic spell you might use, Margie. Ted loves the Beatles, right? So why don't you make him say 'I hate the Beatles' three times. That way he proves himself to really want to be old again. Then maybe you'll make him turn around three times, fall down into a trance — something like that — and he'll be old again."

The imp made Ted turn three handsprings instead of merely turning about. Otherwise, she left the spell intact. While he was following her instructions, she giggled and ran off. Ted, on the floor in his retransformation trance, shook his head to clear it and then slowly got up. But not all the way, because he was once again a bent, broken-down ex-rock star. He hobbled off, playing his guitar in slow motion, and gave us our curtain line: "Let it be, man, let it be."

We now had the outline of a complete show, but as the evening of the performance came closer, I began to worry. I felt I had not allowed enough time for rehearsing the show adequately all the way through, improvisation or no improvisation. The children, to my mind, were too uncertain about what they were going to say and do. The show seemed too diffuse for an audience to understand. I kept them late on the Saturday before the show night, to go over it again. Some of the children became bored with the repetition and began fidgeting; some even wandered away during the rehearsal. I found myself shouting at them.

"It's your show!" I told them. But I implicitly contradicted myself. "It's not good enough yet. It's not ready."

Randy talked to me about this, sensing what was happening, namely, that my ego was getting involved. I was worried that the show would be poor and reflect badly on me.

Younger and less involved with the success-failure syndrome than I was, Randy reminded me that it indeed was the children's show, not mine or hers. I resented what she said at first, but listened:

"Even if they goof at the show," she told me, "they've had the experience and fun of making it up. If the workshop really is for the kids, what's the big deal about the show anyway? Why don't we stop rehearsing and just trust them."

We did. And, in my mind, I tried to give the children back their show. At least I was able to say to myself, "Well, here goes nothing!" I think the children sensed my letting go, and it helped them relax.

My problem about the show made me understand better

why people in charge of school programs do the kind of tight presentations described at the beginning of this chapter. Or rather, since tradition is a strong factor too, why they would have a hard time giving such a thing up. Most adults find it difficult to trust children. Most school directors believe that by definition children are not yet trained or organized enough to be responsible for so critical and complex a thing as a public show. Only if he controls the material does a director feel he can control the children. And only if he controls the children can he hope to avoid a "failure." I think now that one reason I was reluctant to give a show in the first place was because I sensed it would be difficult for me to direct something with such a loose structure and not be apprehensive about its outcome in front of an audience. School directors may have the same difficulty I had in realizing fully (or in acting on the realization) that the primary purpose of staging a show is to give the children themselves some valuable and enjoyable experiences. The audience comes second, and so should the director's anxiety and ego.

Not that it isn't understandable that a director is concerned with the degree of perfection of the show he is responsible for. The desire for excellence can be involved as well as a vulnerable ego and, in terms of his career, a person's reputation for effectiveness in such a situation can be important. The main point is that if a director can mute his ego, ambition, perfectionism, or whatever, enough to try a freer form — which simply means trusting the natural expressiveness of children and, if he can, involving himself with them rather than only directing them — it's quite likely he will produce a more enjoyable show. And what better reputation to have than as a catalyst for spontaneity and natural charm in the performances of children?

As for our show, it turned out neither better or worse than our run-throughs — only different. Just before the curtain went up, the usual tremors of excitement and stage fright were running through the cast. Most of them had never been in a show before and I tried to calm them, telling them not to worry, whatever happened was all right, etc. But when the curtain went up, and the spotlight hit them, an almost visible shock wave seemed to roll over them. Some never recovered from the realization that "All those people out there are watching me!" But most did. The sense of achievement they got from the show must have included the satisfaction at having been able to handle their stage fright and to go on from there.

Our imp turned up sick that night. My well-laid plans for a wily *raisonneuse* who would tie everything together went awry. It was all Margie could do to get through the mechanics of her part. At least, she had been trouper enough to show up, for which we were all grateful.

From my backstage position, it seemed to me that the show at least retained its improvisational feel: some of the things the children did and said that night were brand-new. For instance, Robin and Lucy got into an argument about how short old ladies dresses should be. Sally completely collapsed on her way to her easy chair and the other biddies had to pick her up and seat her. Because the sick imp was barely into her part, Ted had to carry the last scene almost by himself, which he did admirably. Margie's voice was almost inaudible when she gave him the spell to change him back to an old man, so Ted repeated it in a loud, incredulous voice:

"Whaddya mean, turn three somersaults? You must be a *crazy* imp!"

The show got a lot of laughs, which I had forgotten to tell the children to wait for, before proceeding.

The applause at the end was not loud, but when I peeked out from backstage, the faces of the nearest applauders seemed full of tenderness and pleasure. As an encore, the children did a version of our "skipping rope without a rope" exercise. When the curtain opened, the children were sitting around the stage, looking bored.

Somebody said, "Hey, let's skip rope!"

Somebody else said, "Great! I'll get my rope." They began jumping, with Stacey and Betty turning. They jumped in singly, by twos, then threes and then all together. They didn't all jump in unison but their eagerness and energy were there.

After the show, when I talked to people in the audience, they indicated that what had come through best in the main show was the fresh and charming contrast between the slow, infirm "old folks" at the beginning and the quick, electric movements of the children playing themselves at the end. But most of all, they had enjoyed the eager spontaneity of the rope-jumping encore, which had barely been rehearsed at all.

The audience was animated and seemed reluctant to leave. Some lingered a long time, talking in the gym. You could tell they had "seen the children."

/ApTERWORd

This book is based on a series of thirteen-week Saturday morning workshops for children held in 1969 and 1970 at the Metropolitan Duane United Methodist Church at 13th Street and 7th Avenue in New York City. The workshops — of which I was the director — were made possible by a grant to the church from a parishioner, a black woman of moderate means who now lives in Atlanta. This woman desired, anonymously, to fund a free, integrated theater workshop for children of elementary school age. I never talked to the woman myself, but I gathered from Dr. David Giles, pastor of the church until late 1969, that her purpose was to give black and white children an opportunity to work and play together in a creative format, and to help black children in particular develop better feelings about themselves through theater activities. I would guess, however, that the woman would not have made the grant were it not for her faith in Dr. Giles himself. The warmth of this man, and his great interest in children, must have reassured her that her money and her dream were in good hands.

The church had an excellent physical setup for such a workshop project. There was a small but adequately equipped stage in Duane Hall, the lowest floor of the church and the most versatile. It most resembles a small gym at first glance, but it is easily convertible into a ballroom, an art gallery, a dining room (the kitchen adjoins) or, by setting up folding chairs in front of the stage, an auditorium or theater.

I was urged to apply as director of the new project by Janet Fisher, a friend and former Rockland County neighbor who attended the church. Janet knew of my seminars in drama, film and writing for junior and senior high school students, conducted under the auspices of the Community Resources Pool in the county. The latter was an enrichment program originally founded by Betty Friedan and carried on by Melinda Talkington, who recruited people from the arts and sciences, as well as from business and the professions, to give Saturday morning seminars in their specialties. The seminar leaders designed their own courses, in subjects of their own choosing. It's supposed to be difficult to motivate teen-agers to give up their free time to attend anything regularly, especially educational events, but a remarkable number devoted their Saturday mornings to these seminars.

The Resources program, which used the local high school's classrooms and auditorium, enjoyed the cooperation of the public school system, but was completely independent of it. At least, for quite a while. Eventually, and perhaps inevitably, it was incorporated into the system. This was its death knell, because it then lost its exemption from scholastic restrictions and requirements, as well as the excitement of being "outside the Establishment." Losing this, it slowly lost its attraction for both the seminar leaders and the students.

I was involved in the program for a number of years. Although I presently make my living in the business world, I have a Master of Fine Arts degree in dramatic arts and literature from Columbia and have been active in various ways through the years in theater and films. My seminars had such titles as "Today We Improvise" and "Making the Scene," and the children were eager and responsive. The whole experience made me realize how much satisfaction I derive from working in this field.

I left the Resources Pool in 1968. Knowing I had done so, and after convincing me that I would work well with a younger group, Janet Fisher set up an appointment with Dr. Giles and the church theater committee, headed by Joyce Hunter. I presented the outline of a program to them, and was later informed I had been selected as director. Members of the workshop were chosen from among the children of church members and from children in the neighborhood. I myself brought a few children (including my own, at their insistence). The group as it shaped up was satisfyingly mixed, as the book attests: black and white, lower and middle class, with a number of intellectual levels represented, and a variety of personalities. Later, through the generosity of Mr. and Mrs. Samuel Gruber of New York City, I was authorized to hire a paid assistant for the workshop. This I did with the cooperation of Professors Lowell and Nancy Swortzell and Professor Milton Polsky of NYU's program in educational theater.

"How we are educated by children and by animals!" exclaims Martin Buber in *I And Thou*. The children (no animals were allowed, except pretend ones) of the workshop proved educators for everyone involved in it: Parents of workshop children often remarked with surprise on the various (mostly positive) ways the workshop activities affected their children's school progress — as well as enlivened home life. Several members of the church, oriented to traditional church and school performances, couldn't get over the spontaneity and freshness manifested in the children's semi-improvised shows. (These were given at the end of each thirteen-week workshop cycle, in conjunction with a Wednesday night church dinner social.)

"Such talented children!" was the typical comment, where-upon I always replied that they were no more talented than any comparable group of children, but that we *were* trying to help them be freer.

The workshops were educational also in the sense that they taught us all just how much noneducators can do in aid of education. The founder and funder of the program was a woman who simply wanted to help children find some means to express and feel good about themselves. The man who moved it forward, Dr. Giles, was a churchman who had long wanted to launch some kind of enrichment program for children. (Dr. Paul Otto, who succeeded Dr. Giles as pastor of the church, continued the program.) The committee who watched over the workshop and helped me unknot some of the inevitable problems, was composed of two housewives and mothers, a musician, a puppeteer and a comic-book cartoonist. And I myself, not a professional teacher, directed it.

The point is that all of us were outside the formal educational milieu, but each of us was able to partake of that special satisfaction that comes from giving children who would not otherwise have it a creative learning experience. This is certainly not to argue that education should be left to amateurs, but only to say that anyone really interested in children can contribute something to their educational progress, and this contribution can be something children need but do not get in school. The reason that the Resources Pool was so successful, in my opinion, was that the artist or businessman or other professional opened the door for the child to a part of life he would never experience in the classroom: the life in the world as the lay teacher had lived it. The seminar leader distilled the best of what he had learned from his experience in his particular field and gave it to the children. More important, perhaps, each professional was allowed to teach what he loved and what he wanted most to communicate.

In my own case, it is only now that I feel I have something to teach the young, and know what and how I want to teach them. The workshop experiences brought back to me some of my own feelings in childhood, striking something almost forgotten but most important to me. I was brought up in a children's home in the Midwest, during the depression years. In this institution, about forty children were in the charge of a woman superintendent. This woman was so afraid of children, she believed she could manage them only through intimidation, the suffusion of guilt, and the suppression of our private lives and dreams. Perhaps, as is often true with such people, she was most afraid of the child remaining in herself. Fortunately for us, she never completely defeated that child. Although she went to great pains to set herself up as a monolith of discipline and right thinking, "embarrassing" feelings kept surging to the surface to blast this role to pieces. Her criticisms nearly always became diatribes, which often led to fits of weeping. She was also very sentimental and capable of an almost instantaneous change of mood. Such characteristics made it possible for us not to have to take her completely seriously, and we found large holes in the official discipline to wiggle through.

However, I was enough intimidated by her — and suffered enough from the boredom, regimentation and lack of privacy in institutional life — to seek escape in any kind of fantasy I could find — at the movies and inside myself, in the theater in my own head. Again fortunately, the other children wouldn't let me escape very far into my private world. I was a pretty good second baseman, for one thing. They also discovered I was a good mimic, the best animal imitator in the Home. This talent was revealed (to myself as well as them) at a party given for the Home children by the local Rotary Club. There was a contest in animal imitations. I remember the mingled pride and panic I felt when I overheard the contest judges, who were meeting in the kitchen, agree that I was the winner. ("The kid with the big ears, you know, who did the good horse . . .") I had sneaked into the kitchen to eavesdrop on the judges and, when I heard their verdict, rushed back into our big mess hall where the other children were waiting for the outcome. Another boy, my best friend, tripped me and I went down on my face in the middle of the floor, an indescribable heap of pain, fear of exposure and triumph. My prize was Lord Charnwood's *Lincoln*.

The older boys also knew I had good ideas and felt they needed me to help them make up their secret spook-and-sex shows, which they put on for a select invited audience of budding Home girls, after lights out.

Thus I learned the importance, particularly to a child of a barren and/or humiliating background, of creating your own world, of pretending things, of the satisfaction in shaping your fantasies for public view and acclaim. I know what this means to a child's self-esteem and emotional equilibrium.

My growing-up experiences also gave rise to a private dream, a personal version of the myth of turning bad into good, of transforming Furies into Benevolent Ones. In this dream, institutions would condone a child's secret life, value it, and encourage its expression, rather than — as in my case — trying to stamp it out or scorn its special quality. The church workshop described in the book epitomizes this dream: an institution, its staff and members working together, giving a group of children the means, the encouragement and the freedom to be themselves, to learn about themselves and to express themselves.

Since such a workshop project encourages personal achievement in disadvantaged children and thus increases their valuation of themselves — and since it is an activity which promotes a child's inner freedom within a controlling, but very attractive structure — it would seem an excellent (and inexpensive) undertaking for other kinds of modern institutions: community action and recreation groups, socially conscious corporations and labor unions, children's homes, as well as churches and schools. Little is required beyond some professional direction, a place to meet that will let fantasies and ideas come alive, and a strong enthusiasm for children. If this comes under the heading of special pleading, so be it. Children today need all of that they can get.

178